Foreword by the Parliamentary Under Secretary of State for the Environment Sir Paul Beresford MP

The Government's approach to an environmental strategy was first published in the 1990 White Paper 'This Common Inheritance' and has been developed and reported on annually. One of the main supporting principles of our environmental policies is that decisions or actions which could have an adverse affect on the environment should be based on the best possible information and analysis of risks. It is important, therefore, that proper assessments of the risks to the environment are prepared and that we act responsibly by taking precautionary action where it is justified.

Risk of harm to our life, possessions and surroundings is a part of everyday life. Continuing progress to improve the quality of our lives can create new risks which need to be balanced with the benefits. We cannot live in a totally risk free environment but we can try to manage risk.

The techniques of risk assessment and risk management for environmental protection are in their early development. One of the important points made in this guide is that by approaching the problem systematically we shall avoid many mistakes and, by recording carefully how we make our assessments, we shall be able to learn from the mistakes we are bound to make.

This guide is a first attempt to explore some of the underlying principles of assessing environmental risks. It expands on some of the issues in the earlier DOE publications 'Policy Appraisal and the Environment' and 'Environmental Appraisal in Government Departments'.

The guide is intended primarily for policy makers in the public sector but may also be of interest to the generalist reader. Its publication fulfils a commitment in 'This Common Inheritance. UK Annual Report 1995' Fourth Year Report' and contributes to the UK's sustainable development policy.

June 1995

iii

Contents

Chapter 1: Introduction and Definitions

Introduction

1.1   This guide is about assessing and managing risks, particularly environmental risks, in a systematic way as a contribution to the UK's sustainable development strategy. That strategy was published in 1994[1]. It used the widely quoted definition for sustainable development:

"development that meets the needs of the present without compromising the ability of future generations to meet their own needs"[2].

First amongst its principles for action was that:

"decisions should be based on the best possible scientific information and analysis of risks".

It saw risk assessment as helping to take decisions under uncertainty:

"Risk assessment is one of the great challenges in sustainable development policy; the best available science is required to identify the hazards and their potential consequences, and to weigh up the degree of uncertainty. Where appropriate (for example, where there is uncertainty combined with the possibility of the irreversible loss of valued resources), actions should be based on the precautionary principle if the balance of likely costs and benefits justifies it. Even then the action taken and the costs incurred should be in proportion to the risk. Action justified on the basis of the precautionary principle can be thought of as an insurance premium that everyone pays to protect something of value."

This guide attempts to explore some of the underlying principles. It is intended for the generalist reader who is interested in the subject without wanting a full-blown textbook, and for policy makers and managers who need to ensure they can set guidelines for a risk assessment and can critically appraise what is presented to them.

[1] *Sustainable Development. The UK Strategy.* Cm 2426, HMSO, 1994. ISBN 0-10-124262-X
[2] *Our Common Future:* the report of the World Commission on Environment and Development (the "Brundtland Commission"). Oxford University Press, 1987. ISBN 0-19-282080-X

1.2   Nearly every activity has hazards associated with it but it would be unlikely to be under consideration unless it were expected to yield a net benefit. The costs, consequences and benefits need to be considered alongside each other to judge whether the intended course of action will result in risks that are tolerable. If the risks are too high, the intended course of action should be modified and the risks reassessed until a tolerable result is obtained. Only at that stage is it possible to decide whether the benefits justify the costs. This iterative process entails its own substantial burdens.

1.3   In many cases the risks and benefits affect only the individual decision maker whereas in other cases the decision maker's actions will affect other people in ways which are not reflected in prices: this is particularly so for environmental resources such as air, water and soil which are held in common stewardship. Moreover, because we depend on the environment and the health of the ecosystem for our own security and that of future generations, and because we are still learning about the complex inter-relationships that maintain its functions, it is necessary to take particular care about possible harm to the environment and ecosystems, especially where there is potential for irreparable damage whose cost may not be calculable (at least for the present, although valuation techniques are developing all the time). These are among the reasons why this guide treats the concepts of risk assessment and management in the wider context of the needs of human health and the environment, and the commitment to sustainable development made at the UN Conference on Environment and Development, Rio de Janeiro, 1992 (the Earth Summit).

1.4   The 1990 White Paper "This Common Inheritance"[3] set out the main principles which underlie the Government's approach to an environmental strategy. In 1991, a guide for government departments was published entitled "Policy Appraisal and the Environment"[4] and this was followed in June 1994 by "Environmental Appraisal in Government Departments"[5] which looks at how government departments have used and applied the techniques described in the 1991 guide. "Policy Appraisal and the Environment" addressed in part the questions of risk and risk assessment. This guide expands on some of those issues and looks at the entirety of environmental risk assessment.

---

[3] *This Common Inheritance. Britain's Environmental Strategy.* Cm 1200, HMSO, 1990. ISBN 0-10-112002-8.

[4] *Policy Appraisal and the Environment.* Department of the Environment, HMSO, 1991. ISBN 0-11-752487-5.

[5] *Environmental Appraisal in Government Departments.* Department of the Environment, HMSO, 1994. ISBN 0-11-752915-X.

An overview of the terms

1.5   Risk assessment is the structured gathering of the information available about risks and the forming of a judgement about them. Risk management involves using these data to make and implement decisions about risk based on the balance between the costs and benefits (specifically including the environmental costs and benefits) for a range of options that deliver the intended course of action. The communication of the scale and elements of risk to those involved is a key part of a risk management strategy. The structured approach to risk assessment and management recommended here is intended to bring environmental risk assessment more closely in line with risk analysis techniques used in other areas. One aim of this structured approach is to gain a wider acceptance of a common set of principles.

1.6   The vocabulary of the subject suffers from two particular difficulties. The first is that the subject appears to be non-technical because its words are used, sometimes interchangeably, in everyday speech: it is difficult therefore to maintain a consistent technical use of the words. The second is that numerous groups of specialists are accustomed to their own definitions. A first essential therefore is to establish some definitions which are consistent with one another and cause as little difficulty as possible to those with different backgrounds in risk assessment and risk management.

1.7   Some publications refer to the so-called "Rio definitions" incorporated in Commission Directive 93/67/EEC[6], which lays down principles for assessment of risks to man and the environment of substances notified in accordance with Council Directive 67/548/EEC. The title "Rio definitions" conveys the impression that they should be the starting point for this guide. That is not the case: the Rio definitions are designed to deal with chemical substances in the environment and are restricted in scope: they are not suitable for dealing with all intended courses of action encompassing such activities as construction, manufacture, or the release of genetically modified organisms. The definitions, as set out in the Directive, are given in Appendix 1 to the Glossary in Annex 1. A coherent set of definitions for this guide is developed below.

Definitions

1.8   This guide draws on the definitions of hazard, risk and risk assessment and management set out in the Royal Society's 1992 report "Risk: Analysis, Perception and Management"[7] which updated their previous publication of 1983. The following definitions are used:

---

[6] *EC Directive 93/67/EEC*. Official Journal of the European Communities, L227, 8 September 1993. HMSO.

[7] *Risk: Analysis, Perception and Management*. Royal Society, 1992. ISBN 0-85403-467-6

Hazard: a <u>property</u> or <u>situation</u> that in particular circumstances could lead to harm;

Consequences: the adverse effects or harm as the result of realising a hazard which cause the quality of human health or the environment to be impaired in the short or longer term.

Risk: a combination of the probability, or frequency, of occurrence of a defined hazard and the magnitude of the consequences of the occurrence.

Probability: is the mathematical expression of chance (for instance, 0.20, equivalent to a 20 per cent or a one in five chance), wherever this usage is possible but in many cases it can be no more than a prospect which can be expressed only qualitatively. The definition applies to the occurrence of a particular event in a given period of time or as one among a number of possible events.

1.9　Applying the everyday meaning of estimation and evaluation to the defined meaning of risk leads to further terms and definitions:

Risk estimation: is concerned with the outcome or consequences of an intention taking account of the probability of occurrence;

Risk evaluation: is concerned with determining the significance of the estimated risks for those affected: it therefore includes the element of risk perception;

Risk perception: is the overall view of risk held by a person or group and includes both feeling and judgement;

Risk assessment: consists of <u>risk estimation</u> and <u>risk evaluation</u>. This definition of risk assessment, by incorporating risk evaluation, goes beyond that in the Commission Directive 93/67/EEC.

1.10　Up to now, this guide has used the term 'intended course of action' to cover a wide range of possible actions that should be subject to a risk assessment. Hereafter the guide will refer to 'intention':

Intention: includes the manufacture and use of a substance; the creation, testing and release of an organism; the construction or demolition of some artifact or scheme; an operation or process; any combination of intentions: and, for all intentions, taking account of inputs, useful and waste products, by-products and emissions.

When considering an intention, one possibility is to do nothing. However, a decision to do nothing is as much a decision as one to do something and the consequences should be addressed in the same way as for other intentions.

1.11 Having assessed the risks associated with an intention, there is the question of what to do about the risks. This is the issue of risk management:

Risk management: is the process of implementing decisions about accepting or altering risks.

Risk management should be based on the assessment of the various costs and benefits stemming from possible actions. One possible benefit of risk management is the reduction of environmental risk rather than direct financial benefit.

1.12 The commitment to sustainable development is a principal reason for performing risk assessment and risk management. A definition was given in paragraph 1.1:

Sustainable development: is "development that meets the needs of the present without compromising the ability of future generations to meet their own needs"[2].

1.13 The simple logical sequence of steps from intention to risk management is set out in Diagram 1 at the end of this chapter. A more elaborate version of this diagram is to be found at the end of Chapter 4 in Diagram 2; it takes account of the feedback process that results from assessments or decisions made following the various steps of the process.

1.14 The principal terms defined in paragraphs 1.7 to 1.10 are illustrated in the box over page. The paragraph dealing with risk management deliberately refers to an option which most people would consider unthinkable: it is included to make the serious point that inbuilt or implicit assumptions may cause certain options to be ruled in or out.

---

[2] *Our Common Future:* the report of the World Commission on Environment and Development (the "Brundtland Commission"). Oxford University Press, 1987. ISBN 0-19-282080-X

A SIMPLISTIC ILLUSTRATION OF THE PRINCIPAL TERMS

Intention: to leave Nelson's column in place as it is, unless a risk assessment reveals intolerable risks.

One **hazard** is that stones of a particular size and weight under certain circumstances might be dislodged and fall; a <u>consequence</u> is that a passer-by might be struck and killed or injured by falling masonry.

Risk estimation might follow the lines that the probability per unit time that a stone will fall is very low whilst the probability that if it does fall it will hit a passer-by is low most of the time; the magnitude of the consequence is high for the person affected but overall the risk to the passer-by is estimated to be low.

Risk evaluation determines whether the risk is significant in relation, for example, to other risks to pedestrians in Trafalgar Square and taking account of perception *ie* the fact that people do not perceive a risk of being hit by a falling stone in Trafalgar Square.

The **risk assessment** would probably be that the risk was negligible.

If the risk were judged to be significant, **risk management** would lead to consideration of actions taken to reduce the level of risk and the cost of such actions. Those actions and the reduction in risk thereby achieved would be subject to a like process of evaluation. Possible actions are: to demolish the column (for which there is the difficulty of valuing the loss of benefit of a Trafalgar Square without a Nelson's column); to strengthen the column; to leave the column alone but to erect fencing to preclude people from the area around the base of the column; to manage the risk by monitoring and maintaining Nelson's column; or to leave it alone. The last two actions should take account of the possible development of a greater risk due to, for example, underground works or vibration caused by heavy lorries.

Types of risk

1.15 This guide will be applicable to the risks associated with substances and organisms; construction and demolition; operating and processing; and inputs, products, emissions and wastes. The guide will be applicable both to risks that arise from discrete events and to risks that arise from continuous processes.

1.16 Some of these types of risk are the concern of particular organisations: for example, the Health and Safety Executive is concerned with risks arising at the workplace. Such organisations will be a valuable source of expertise whether through their publications or by enquiry. Annex 6 lists a number of such organisations and gives a brief description of their particular areas of expertise that are relevant to this guide.

1.17 In writing this guide there was a choice between a generalised overview of risk assessment and risk management for sustainable development, and a guide which focused more narrowly on their application to toxic substances and organisms in relation to sustainable development. The overview was chosen because to date most of the work on risk assessment and risk management has been restricted to effects on human health; rather less has been done in relation to the environment; and little has set in the context of sustainable development. As will be seen, taking account of sustainable development is difficult but the hope is that the overview provided by this guide will complement earlier more specific work, show how it should fit into the broader picture, and help build up the techniques needed to take account of sustainable development.

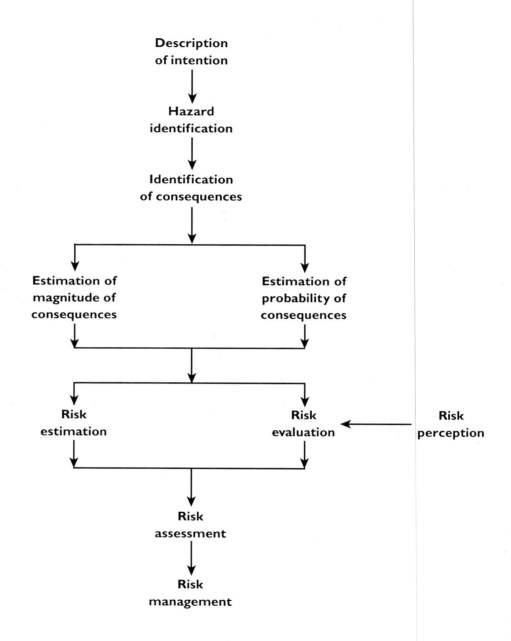

Diagram 1: From intention to risk management

Chapter 2: Why carry out an Environmental Risk Assessment?

Aspects outside this chapter

2.1   This section concentrates on risk assessment in an environmental context. More general aspects of policy appraisal for environmental protection, that is, aspects other than environmental risk assessment, are covered in the companion guide "Policy Appraisal and the Environment"[1]. The legal requirements for environmental risk assessment may be obtained by referring to one of the computer-based legal search systems such as "Lexis" and by seeking expert advice. One reason for seeking legal advice is that legal definitions of terms are often specific to the interpretation of the particular legal instrument in which they appear. Moreover, in the commercial and industrial sectors, compliance with legal requirements may often be a compelling reason for carrying out an environmental risk assessment.

The nature of risk assessments

2.2   People perform numerous simple risk assessments every day in order to be able to make some sort of judgement about the risk associated with a particular action. These risk assessments are often intuitive, involving some considerable understanding of the possible outcomes, their severity and probabilities. Simple examples are safety risks in crossing the road, health risks of smoking or prolonged exposure to the sun, and so on. This chapter considers this familiar process as a whole, and Chapters 3 and 4 then consider parts of the process in more detail.

2.3   Risk assessment as a formal process should be carried out in advance of an intention (although a retrospective risk assessment might be necessary if a previously unidentified risk were brought to light). It consists of an information gathering exercise followed by a prognosis about the outcome. It can be an expensive exercise and the resources used should not be disproportionate to the risk: the resources appropriate to a particular intention will become clearer as the assessment develops. Quite often it will be proper not to pursue certain theoretical possibilities because experience and knowledge of similar cases show that the risks

---

[1] *Policy Appraisal and the Environment.* Department of the Environment, HMSO, 1991. ISBN 0-11-752487-5.

are negligible. However, the basis of such decisions within the risk assessment should be recorded because new knowledge should lead to a reassessment and may alter previous judgements. Monitoring the actual outcome can help determine the quality of the risk assessment, though where predicted risks are low the time taken to accumulate enough data to confirm the estimate may be very long. Nevertheless, if the assessment did not take account of all the relevant factors, this will often become evident from monitoring. Subsequent assessments of similar intentions are improved if the monitoring results are then fed into those assessments. The role of monitoring is more fully developed in Chapter 6.

Uncertainty

2.4   Most decisions have to be taken on the basis of incomplete information and sometimes in circumstances of uncertainty. When potential damage is uncertain and may be significant it is necessary to act on the **precautionary principle**. How that principle should be applied is described fully in Chapter 5: it applies not only in advance of an intention but also to corrective action after an intention has been effected if a previously unforeseen possibility of damage arises. It is particularly pertinent to corrective action that the *Rio Declaration*[2] says

> **"Where there are threats of serious or irreversible damage, lack of full scientific certainty shall not be used as a reason for postponing cost-effective measures to prevent environmental degradation."**

The question of what degree of damage is "significant" is discussed in Chapter 4 under the sections on risk evaluation and risk perception.

2.5   As paragraph 2.4 suggests, the precautionary principle may militate against undertakings such as the manufacture of a new product that might have been undertaken if their effects were known with greater certainty. "This Common Inheritance"[3] says

> **"Where the state of our planet is at stake, the risks can be so high and the costs of corrective action so great that prevention is better and cheaper than cure. We must analyse the possible benefits and costs of both action and inaction".**

2.6   Risk assessment may help in applying the precautionary principle but, where the risks and uncertainties are very large, (as with global change issues), it is important to avoid being misled by the formal framework of risk assessment into thinking that the quantification of risk is more accurate than it really is. In such cases risk analysis should be undertaken with a range of well documented input assumptions, to

---

[2] *Rio Declaration on Environment and Development*, 1992. ISBN 9-21-100509-4.

[3] *This Common Inheritance. Britain's Environmental Strategy.* Cm 1200. HMSO. 1990. ISBN 0-10-112002-8.

examine the sensitivity of the results, and due weight should be given to the results of more ad-hoc analyses and assessments.

The starting point problem

2.7   There are those who are opposed to change for fear of possible adverse consequences whilst discounting potential benefits; and others who are in favour of change for its perceived benefits and are blind to or ignore possible adverse consequences. There is no clear cut right and wrong in such matters and no means of checking past choices by testing the alternatives. The primaeval environment was rather hostile to mankind with the result that most people now live in an environment which has been highly modified over the centuries. The environment we inhabit is how things happen to be but we do not know if it is sustainable in the long term or if it is necessarily better than what it might be changed into. Simply to maintain things as they are rules out the possibility of benefiting from an intention but is not necessarily a recipe for sustainable development. However, in considering whether any change brought about by fulfilling an intention is harmful, we can be certain that, considered in isolation, the loss of non-renewable resources and the loss of genetic diversity through the destruction of species constitute harm; and such considerations will weigh heavily in any assessment of risk. However, such losses could result in other benefits by stimulating the search for alternatives.

Risks to people

2.8   In the restricted context of direct risks to people, the intuitive but, as will become clear, logically unsustainable starting point is the overriding need to preserve human life. If the need to preserve a human life were overriding there would be no limit on the resources devoted to that purpose but, given that resources are necessarily limited, the unlimited provision of resources to that life would be to the detriment of other lives whose needs ought also to be considered overriding. It follows that explicitly or implicitly a price must be put on human life and the quality of life and that risk assessment must acknowledge and design to a specific probability for the preservation of human life. This requires a knowledge of human physiology and pathology in judging the effects on mankind of a substance, intended action or system. However, this is not always easy. For example, in the particular case of assessing the risk from chemical substances, a crucial difficulty is that the dose (or exposure)-response curve is commonly not known, especially at low levels of exposure (see Glossary). Despite the difficulties every reasonable effort should be made to evaluate the impacts.

A problem peculiar to environmental risks

2.9   The term 'critical natural capital' describes parts of the environment which are vital to the continued functioning of natural systems. In circumstances where an intention might jeopardise the critical natural capital, the preservation of the environment might be judged to be paramount. Whereas the concept of critical natural capital has been applied to a particular species (for example, the South American condor) which might be unable to survive if its numbers dropped too low, some biologists dispute the validity of the concept applied to any but a limited ecosystem. Whatever the merits of the concept and the ways in which it should be applied, the judgement required is that of striking a balance between positive environmental utilisation and potential environmental degradation, bearing in mind the needs of future generations.

Risks to the environment

2.10   Consideration of risk to humans, as opposed to other organisms, is rather different from the assessment of risks to the environment. Humans are but a part of the environment, which has many dimensions: air, soil and water — the non-living environment (although some people prefer to consider soil as part of the living environment); the living environment of animals, plants and microbes; the ecosystems and habitats in which those organisms live; and the man-made environment, such as towns and cities. An environmental risk assessment therefore involves judging the effects of an action or event on many varied components. The dose-response rate problem mentioned in paragraph 2.8 is equally true for non-human facets of the environment.

2.11   Not only is the environment a many faceted system but there is no easily defined measure of what constitutes damage to the environment. The Environmental Protection Act 1990 (the Act) gives different definitions according to context. In relation to polluting substances, the Act defines pollution of the environment as the release from any process of substances which are capable of causing harm to man or any other living organisms supported by the environment. For genetically modified organisms (GMOs) the Act defines damage to the environment as the presence of GMOs which have escaped or been released and are capable of causing harm to the living organisms supported by the environment. Damage may therefore be caused to organisms directly or indirectly, immediately or over time, as a result of effects on the air, soil and water which support organisms. In the Act, harm means harm to the health of living organisms or other interference with the ecosystems of which they form part.

2.12   In other words, any effect on any organism might constitute harm and imagination and judgement is needed to select appropriate criteria for the conditions under consideration. Harm includes harm to a person's property or offence to their senses. Since any action will necessarily produce some environmental change which strictly could be considered to be harmful, this guide aims to set out indicators for assessing whether the effects are significant. Measuring the significance of harm will be easier if clear and quantifiable measures of environmental quality are available that allow measurement of changes in environmental and ecological baselines. However, environmental and ecological systems are inherently variable and subject to continual dynamic change albeit slow. The concept of a baseline may be more simplistic than practicable in all but the most clear cut cases such as the draining of wetland: it may be more pertinent to consider whether effects are outside normal environmental variations.

2.13   For many activities environmental impact is an "externality", that is, effects on it are not automatically reflected in the cost of carrying out the intention. If a risk assessment for such intentions revealed significant effects on the environment then one way of ensuring that the externality was not ignored might be formal regulatory control of such intentions by the introduction of new legislation. It is taken as read that such regulatory control should be well targeted to ensure that the costs of compliance are commensurate with the benefits achieved from the reduction of risk, with the aim of ensuring minimum burdens on industry and other operators. Regulation is only one of a number of ways in which the desired end may be achieved: others are discussed in "Making Markets Work for the Environment"[4]. That document makes it clear that the Government is committed to using, where practicable, economic instruments rather than regulation.

2.14   The assessment of risk, the accompanying assessment of costs and benefits, and the decision whether to go ahead with an intention imply a judgement of what degree of harm is tolerable, always bearing in mind that risk cannot always be identified or quantified. The Health and Safety Executive have considered the issue of what is a tolerable risk. Their paper "The Tolerability of Risk from Nuclear Power Stations"[5] suggests

> **"Tolerability" does not mean "acceptability". It refers to a willingness to live with a risk so as to secure certain benefits and in the confidence that it is being properly controlled. To tolerate a risk means that we do not regard it as negligible or something we might ignore, but rather as something we need to keep under review and reduce still further if and as we can. For a risk to be "acceptable" on the other hand means that for the purposes of life or work, we are prepared to take it pretty well as it is.**

---

[4] *Making Markets Work for the Environment.* Department of the Environment, HMSO, 1993, ISBN 0-11-752852-8

[5] *The Tolerability of Risk from Nuclear Power Stations.* HSE, HMSO, 1992, ISBN 0-11-886368-1.

Conclusions

2.15   The discussion leads to the following list of reasons for carrying out an environmental risk assessment:

- ★ Our duty of stewardship and commitment to sustainable development requires proper assessment of environmental risks;

- ★ Analysis may facilitate a judgement and allow a more quantified judgement to be made;

- ★ Inability to make a quantified judgement should not be used to avoid doing a risk assessment and it may indicate where more information should be sought;

- ★ The identification of uncertainty and serious potential damage may indicate the need to invoke the precautionary principle or to so modify the intention as to render the risks tolerable;

- ★ Analysis may indicate where regulatory measures are needed;

- ★ A prognosis of an outcome provides the basis for monitoring and control; and

- ★ Recorded analysis facilitates a reappraisal in changed circumstances or the light of new knowledge.

Moreover, there may be the legal or commercial reasons referred to in paragraph 2.1.

Chapter 3: The Five Stages Leading up to Risk Estimation

Introduction

3.1 It is convenient to divide the whole process leading up to risk management into two parts for ease of handling and comprehension. This chapter deals with the various stages leading up to risk estimation but does not include it. The divide has been made at that point because the preliminary stages can be considered separately whereas risk estimation requires a synthesis of the preceding stages. Risk estimation, risk evaluation, their combination in risk assessment, and risk management are treated in Chapter 4.

The five stages leading up to risk estimation

3.2 Before an environmental risk assessment can even begin, it is first necessary to make clear what is to be assessed. This part of the process comprises five stages:

1. Description of intention;

2. Hazard identification;

3. Identification of consequences;

4. Estimation of magnitude of consequences; and

5. Estimation of probability of consequences.

Some general points

3.3 At every stage of a risk assessment and risk management study, assumptions should be made explicit so that any further review can establish whether the situation has changed sufficiently to warrant modification. A formal record will encourage the review and monitoring process with the benefits that can be expected from it (See Chapter 6).

3.4 The problem of uncertainty was alluded to in paragraph 2.4. There is no general solution to the problem of uncertainty and the solution to be adopted will have to be made and justified step by step in the prevailing circumstances. This is an area where good records of the basis of decisions can be particularly useful because developments in experience or knowledge may later permit an estimate of what was previously uncertain.

3.5   Many intentions will affect a number of interests and the decision on what to do is bound to favour one rather than another or at least appear to do so to one of the interests concerned. There is no clear cut way to deal with such problems when the interests are unquantifiable and qualitatively not too far apart. Any decision is bound to be criticised, so good records are important to show that due attention was paid to the various concerns and that the chosen decision was made in good faith and was justifiable in terms of the knowledge then obtainable.

3.6   The concept of hazard is not relevant to aesthetic values which are not considered in this guide. Nevertheless, aesthetic values should not be ignored when identifying consequences. The probability of their occurrence may be quantifiable but their magnitude will be debatable.

Stage 1: Description of intention

3.7   The quality of any risk assessment is determined by the extent of knowledge of what is to be done and the effects. This may require knowledge of the characteristics of particular substances or organisms, and of each component and stage of intended operations and processes. It will also require knowledge of the pre-existing situation and of the situation that will obtain after completion of the intention. Just how full the description need be will be a matter of judgement. A limited description of operation may be sufficient for safety purposes of well precedented operations in a factory but something much fuller may be needed for the effect of that factory in a particular environment.

3.8   There are four main groups of questions to be answered:

what are the intrinsic physical, chemical, physico-chemical and biological characteristics of the substances, organisms, agents, processes and structures that:

(i)   exist <u>before</u> fulfilling the intention?

(ii)   are to be applied to fulfilling the intention?

(iii) what are the intended individual steps of the entire operation or process, including the intended outcome? and

(iv)   as (i) but <u>after</u> fulfilling the intention?

Of these, (i) and (ii) and therefore (iv) generally relate to intrinsic hazards, whereas (iii) generally relates to operational hazards. In many cases experience will show that a question is irrelevant and it can be set aside after minimal consideration.

3.9   For the particular example of the construction of a new brewing plant, what would be required is an environmental impact assessment. It would describe:

under (i), the physical characteristics of the site, its ecology and hydrology, its social setting, the services;

under (ii), the physico-chemical and biological characteristics of all the individual organisms, nutrients, necessary chemicals, and the products including waste products;

under (iii), all the building or engineering stages from site investigation and clearing the land, through construction and on to eventual demolition; the inputs, not forgetting water and energy; the processes, including all emissions and wastes to air, water, soil etc; and, for both construction and operation, transportation of materials, products and by-products to and from the site; and

under (iv), the same as under (i) in the situation after completion of the intention.

3.10   A hidden benefit of a recorded description of intention is that at any later date it will be possible for other people to tell what was taken into account. For those intimately concerned with a particular intention it is easy to make implicit assumptions or take account of knowledge that will not be known to those reviewing it later. A good statement of intention will facilitate monitoring and feedback and help to distinguish whether discrepancies between pre-estimates and outturn were caused by poor judgement, lack of knowledge or other factors.

3.11   At the stage of describing the intention there should be no attempt to identify or evaluate the consequences: that is part of the next stage. It is the description of intention in the first stage which is a necessary precondition to identifying clearly in the second stage those features that <u>could</u> cause environmental or other harm.

**Stage 2:
Hazard identification**

3.12   In this guide, hazards are defined as properties or circumstances that could give rise to harm. Consider the examples of hazards stemming from the properties of chloro-fluorocarbons (CFCs) and the use of X-radiography.

3.13   CFCs have the advantages of stability and relatively low reactivity with many chemicals. However, they are capable of acting catalytically to deplete stratospheric ozone which protects the earth from harmful ultraviolet radiation. As for X-radiography, its early developers were aware only of its significant potential for benefit. In both cases, the associated hazards became apparent only after the substances or processes had long been in use. These examples point up the importance of undertaking the process of hazard identification at the time an intention is declared and the need to repeat the process in the light of fresh knowledge.

3.14   In some areas hazard identification is relatively well developed: for instance, as regards certain intrinsic properties of chemicals and physical agents such as noise and radiation. It is inevitably a highly technical area. Hazards will include certain physico-chemical properties, flammability, mutagenicity, acute and chronic vertebrate toxicity etc. In some cases structure-activity relationships can be used to predict the hazardous properties of chemicals.

3.15   Looking forward to a later stage of the process, hazard identification often provides a short cut to risk estimation. As an example, by expressing the toxicity of a chemical to a certain fish species in terms of the LC_{50} (the lethal concentration required to kill 50% of the fish), comparisons can be made between different chemicals, and estimates of concentration lead rapidly to the estimation of the magnitude of consequences. The European Commission classifies the environmental effects of chemicals on the basis of the LC_{50} and other specific hazards. However, toxicity testing is a complex subject with many forms of expression which requires expert advice on interpretation.

3.16   Hazards are associated not only with substances, operations and processes but also with organisms. For example, certain microorganisms are pathogenic to humans, other animals or plants; some plants are toxic; and pollen from some plants elicits allergenic responses in some humans. These are fairly well characterised, and therefore identifiable, hazards. Those organisms which are not well characterised may pose difficulties as regards hazard identification.

3.17   Hazard may also be related to location. Different sites may have different hazards. Examples are: geological conditions which could permit pollution of groundwater by leachate from contaminated land; geotechnical conditions for a flood embankment or dam. For such location related hazards, site investigation is an essential precursor to hazard identification.

3.18   The question that needs to be answered in order to derive a first order environmental hazard identification is:

Which of the identified properties of the intended substance, organism, operation, process or undertaking <u>could</u> lead to adverse effects on the environment?

3.19   In particular, answering the question will involve considering the detailed description from Stage 1 in terms of:

* toxicity, immunotoxicity, pathogenicity, mutagenicity, teratogenicity and carcinogenicity;

* potential for long-lived presence in the environment   including the potential to bioaccumulate and bioconcentrate;

* potential for effects on environmental processes such as photosynthesis, the nitrogen and carbon cycles;

* potential for effects on air (including upper atmosphere), water and soil;

* potential for affecting ecosystem function, such as influence on predator/prey relationships or changes in population numbers of the species in an ecosystem;

* potential for causing offence to people or adverse effects on them; and

* potential for accidents.

3.20   The hazards outlined above are necessarily very broad. In any individual case however, the hazards should be as clearly defined as practicable. This will improve the quality of the final risk assessment. An example of a risk assessment for the release of a genetically modified organism is given in Annex 2: it illustrates this chapter and Chapter 4.

3.21   If there is insufficient information to assess whether a specific hazard is present, the assumption for the purpose of working through the remaining stages of the risk assessment should be that the hazard is present. This is no more than an application of the precautionary principle. The set of possible hazards could be very large indeed, so some cautious judgement will be needed about what can be ignored for practical purposes. One approach would be to make a realistic worst case estimate for those components for which the estimate is not affected by uncertainty and then to add a further factor for uncertainty. As knowledge is gained, hazards can be more closely defined and assessed.

3.22   The next part of hazard identification is to ask:

Where, and to what extent, might an operation or process, or the individual stages of an operation, of their nature or through failure cause environmental harm?

The answer requires examination of the individual steps of the operation set down in Stage 1. In the example of the new brewing plant, one such event might be spillage from tankers.

3.23   In many cases, the search for process failures is likely to be appropriate only when intrinsically hazardous properties have been identified. For example, if a flammable chemical is required by a company for an industrial process, one of the associated hazards would be the transportation of that chemical to the plant. In contrast, if bags of yeast are being brought to a brewery the effect of one falling is likely to be no more significant than the risk of any moderately heavy weight.

3.24   There are standard techniques for identifying consequences which can arise from process or operation failures. These techniques include event and fault tree analysis, reliability and failure analysis, and hazard and operability (HAZOP) studies: examples of these techniques are given in Annex 4. They have mainly been used in the context of the assessment of risk to humans but they could be applied to environmental risk assessment, if the potential environmental effects outlined in paragraph 3.19 are used to pinpoint the process hazards. However, such techniques do not have universal application and their suitability for any given circumstances will be a matter of expert judgement.

Stage 3: Identification of consequences

3.25   The potential consequences of an operation are determined in the first place by the hazards identified. A specific consequence arises only if the underlying hazard is realised but that can happen only if the potential receiving environment possesses the necessary characteristics and/or if operational or process failures do indeed take place. This applies to hazardous characteristics of the substance or organism, and of the operation, process or undertaking in normal conditions or failure.

3.26   Wherever possible when dealing with a substance or organism, the exposure of the receiving environment or people to that substance or organism should be estimated, taking account of the different routes by which they might have effect. For people, the routes might include direct inhalation or ingestion, absorption through the skin, ingestion through affected food and water, and so on. Exposure should be considered for the complete life cycle of the substance from manufacture, through use, to final disposal; and similarly for an organism. For exposure associated with a particular site of manufacture or use, such estimates should take account of effects well removed from the site at points downstream, downwind or down aquifer from it. Exposure may be point, local or regional. An example of exposure assessment for a household product in the environment is given in Annex 3.

3.27   Identifying the outcome depends on the combination of the hazard and the characteristics of the potential receiving environment that are relevant to the particular hazard. They might be climate-based, geographical, use-based (such as whether a potentially affected water source is used for drinking purposes), organism/ecosystem-based and so on. The characteristics of that environment may even be such that certain hazards will not be realised.

3.28 Two examples will illustrate paragraph 3.27:

(i) If a virus pathogenic only to zebras is used in a UK veterinary research laboratory, it is virtually impossible that the hazard could be realised outside zoos and wildlife parks, and the risk from that hazard could be considered to be zero.

(ii) An industrial plant which is very noisy will cause offence to people (harm) only if it is located close to areas where people live and work but, it must be remembered, once the industrial plant has been built the continuing hazard of noise may deter people from living near it and may affect non-human life around it.

3.29 The consequences stemming from particular hazards may be very wide-ranging, impacting on the living, and/or the non-living environment. As regards the living environment, it is useful to consider whether the consequences from any one hazard might lead, directly or indirectly, in the short term or the long term, to the following:

★ populations of organisms being displaced or eradicated;

★ a shift in species population numbers, or community composition; and/or

★ endangered species being affected by the operation.

3.30 In this guide, consequence is defined to include the concept of harm. The list of effects in paragraph 3.29 could be, when viewed as outcomes (to use a word without a restrictively defined meaning), harmful or beneficial depending on the direction of change in the particular circumstances. The one exception is a general presumption that the eradication of an organism constitutes harm. One of the tenets of sustainable development is the need to maintain biodiversity; and conversely to accept that where there are many representatives of an organism the local eradication of a few will probably not pose a problem. One reason for maintaining biodiversity is that species that currently are considered harmful may at some future time prove to be beneficial: to classify a species as harmful or beneficial may be to take a view that is valid only at the time.

3.31   The example in the box below illustrates a particular case that accords with the normal assumptions about what constitutes harm. Notwithstanding the definition of consequence and the duty to consider possible consequences, the development of substances and organisms, operations, processes and undertakings is embarked upon for the benefits that are expected. Without benefits, the development would be dropped and the question of assessing potential harmful outcomes would not arise.

> ### THE USE OF DDT
>
> It is now clear that compounds such as DDT accumulate at increasing concentrations throughout the food chain, often causing most damage to the predators, such as falcons, eagles and cormorants, at the upper end of the food chain. While DDT was used extensively, the reproduction capacity of such birds was affected because the females were unable to form normal eggshells, and the number of birds successfully hatched declined. In terms of the criteria in paragraph 3.29 there was a shift in species population numbers: the result of reduced fecundity constituted harm.

3.32   Many operations or the repetition of such operations may have a detrimental effect on the non-living environment. Examples are:

(a)   emissions from chemical plants to air, soil and water;

(b)   extractive industries using finite resources;

(c)   the construction and use of ski lifts on mountains, leading to forest felling and soil erosion;

(d)   changes to coast protection regimes in one area leading to cliff erosion in another; and

(e)   acid rain or black smoke damaging the built environment.

In terms of sustainable development, the first four clearly have the potential to be significant; as for the last, damage to the built environment requires extra resources for repair or replacement and it could also be significant in terms of heritage. If not enough regard is paid to such effects, there may be a case for an enforcement regime of prosecution and penalties.

3.33   A person's senses may be offended. This might be the result of low levels of pollution in the form of noise, smell or poor air and water quality. Such effects have to be taken into account for some aspects of risk assessment but in terms of sustainable development may become relevant only if they occur very widely.

Stage 4: Estimation of magnitude of consequences

3.34   The consequences of a specific hazard being realised are, by definition, harm or adverse effects on human health and/or the environment. In some cases it will be possible to quantify their magnitude and even to assign a monetary value to them. Even when full quantification of consequences is impossible it may be possible to judge the order of magnitude of effects or to adopt a semi-quantitative approach. Every attempt should be made when consequences cannot be known to infer what they might be from the most comparable precedents.

3.35   In making such an estimate, the concept of exposure can be helpful. In the case of a chemical substance, humans may be exposed to it via the air, by breathing it or by skin contact; food; water, by drinking, washing or bathing; or by skin contact. For each route, the exposure analysis should take account of the intensity, duration and extent of exposure. In assessing the significance, it would be necessary to take account of vulnerable groups such as infants, diabetics, asthmatics and so on.

3.36   Consideration of the magnitude of consequences can helpfully be divided into consideration of the living and the non-living environment. For the living environment other than humans, it can be useful to consider the effect that a particular hazard, if realised, could ultimately have on populations of organisms and/or on endangered or beneficial species:

> **Severe:** a significant change in the numbers of one or more species, including beneficial and endangered species, over a short or long term. This might be a reduction or complete eradication of a species, which for some organisms could lead to a negative effect on the functioning of the particular ecosystem and/or other connected ecosystems.

> **Moderate:** a significant change in population densities, but not a change which resulted in total eradication of a species or had any effect on endangered or beneficial species.

> **Mild:** some change in population densities, but without total eradication of other organisms and no negative effects on ecosystem function.

> **Negligible:** no significant changes in any of the populations in the environment or in any ecosystem functions.

3.37 This ranking depends on a broad knowledge of the species present in the receiving environment, as well as the likely effects on those species. Although there is no comprehensive data base providing an inventory of all the species present in any one environment, and the effects of various operations, or chemicals or radiation, on those species, there is a considerable body of information available which can contribute to the estimation. Whilst the magnitude of consequences has been related to species, which we may wish to preserve for themselves alone or for other reasons, species can also be considered as a proxy for functions which should be preserved.

3.38 Complete loss of a species is of prime significance in terms of sustainable development and is qualitatively different from local eradication. It follows that harm to endangered species must be considered serious. Even for a species which is not endangered, loss at the local level would, over and above the undesirable decrease in biodiversity, be likely to affect the immediate ecosystem as well as having knock-on effects on other organisms and ecosystems such as predator/ prey interactions. In such an event, changes would probably not be readily reversible and any recovery of the ecosystem that did take place would be likely to be slow. However, not all species may be needed for the integrity of ecosystem functioning as there is often quite a high degree of redundancy within ecosystems. Even so, the concern about loss of biodiversity would remain in assessing whether a consequence was severe.

3.39 In a case where land is the receiving environment, one approach is first to classify the type of land likely to be affected as, for example, arable agricultural land, lowland bog, deciduous or evergreen wood, urban/industrial etc. For each type of land there will be an associated range of species. The Institute of Terrestrial Ecology have already developed such a land classification on the basis of satellite-derived information about landscape elements and features. For other ultimate receiving environments different methods of classification and different databases will be appropriate.

3.40 Careful consideration of the type of the potential receiving environment in terms of its associated biodiversity and the degree of disturbance it would suffer can give a useful first order approximation for judging whether harm is likely to occur. Two sources of relevant information are the Institute of Terrestrial Ecology's Biological Records Centre which contains records of some 10,000 species and the National Vegetation Classification. Reference to data of this sort should give an indication about the degree of biodiversity in a particular environment and should make an estimation of the magnitude of the environmental consequences of an operation more accessible.

3.41   If the aquatic environment is the receiving medium, among the appropriate sources of reference would be Her Majesty's Inspectorate of Pollution, the National Rivers Authority, and the Institute for Freshwater Ecology in England and Wales; the River Purification Boards in Scotland; the Department of the Environment for Northern Ireland in Northern Ireland.

3.42   The effects of particular chemicals and physical agents on certain types of organisms may be known. The specialist will be familiar with the standard works of reference: such published data should be used wherever possible in reaching an estimate of the seriousness of the potential outcome. Consideration should be given to whether the organisms for which such data is available might be taken as representative for one component of the ecosystems/habitats/areas likely to be affected by the operation.

3.43   A further consideration relates to the time-scale of events. The ability of the environment to recover may be related to the generation time of the species affected. If an event, or a consequence, is itself very short-lived, the consequences might be very low if regeneration or recolonisation from the surrounding environment could take place fairly rapidly.

3.44   To assess the magnitude of consequences for <u>the non-living environment</u> a similar approach may be taken to that for the living environment:

Severe effects might be irreparable damage to geological features;

Moderate effects might be damage to structures which are present in limited numbers (such as Grade II listed buildings);

Mild effects might be damage to commonplace present day structures which could be repaired; and

Negligible effects might be very slight damage to such structures.

3.45   A further important consideration in assessing the magnitude of the consequences is the scale of the operation, not just in absolute terms but also in relation to the affected environment.

**Stage 5:
Estimation of
probability of
consequences**

3.46   Any estimation of the probability or frequency of a particular intrinsic hazard being realised is likely to be at best semi-quantitative. Such an assessment may be made by judging the substance, organism, operation, process or undertaking against the best available comparison. By contrast, process failure may be more quantifiable because the rate will have been measured and is often included as part of equipment specification or as part of the engineering design parameters. The aim throughout should be to quantify as much as possible so as to reduce the need for judgement and the associated scope for dissent or argument.

3.47   Where quantification is not possible, the probability should at least be expressed as within ranges of order of magnitude for a specified number of events or time period such as 100 years. Ranges would differ according to the nature of the consequence which, for ease of use, might be divided into "high", "medium", "low" and "negligible". The ranges would be deliberately overlapping so as to avoid a threshold value. However, in establishing ranges for a particular event, it is necessary to be absolutely clear what event is being considered. For example, if a factory discharges a chemical into a river, the harm caused will be different in each of the following cases:

the discharge exceeds a certain quantity (but may have nearly no significance if the river is in spate);

the concentration of the chemical in the river exceeds a certain level (but may not be significant except in months when fish are breeding); or

the concentration exceeds a certain level at some point downstream from the discharge, say, a water company's abstraction point (in which case, the significance may depend on the flow at the discharge point, circumstances in other areas and on such factors as whether the company needs to abstract water just at the time when the discharge concentration is passing its abstraction point).

3.48   The appropriate values for the ranges will vary according to what is under consideration and who is doing the considering. Thus a bungee jumper may consider a probability of 0.001 for a fatal accident on one jump as low, whereas the public might consider that same value as high, if applied to a particular value of emission of radiation from a nuclear power station. This issue of perception of risk is dealt with more fully in Chapter 4.

Summary

3.49 The principal points made in this chapter are set out below.

★ At every stage, assumptions should be made explicit and recorded.

★ There can be no general solution to weighing up the balance of uncertainties.

★ The intrinsic characteristics of the situation before and after fulfilling the intention should be described taking account of a sufficiently full description of the component steps of fulfilling the intention.

★ The process for identifying hazards must be appropriate to the nature of the intention but take account of the possibility of unintended events.

★ The identification of consequences depends on the combination of hazard and the relevant characteristics of the receiving environment.

★ If the magnitude of consequences cannot be estimated directly, it should be inferred from comparable precedents.

★ In estimating magnitudes of consequences, it may be helpful to consider separately the non-human living environment.

★ Loss of species or function is of prime significance in assessing the magnitude of consequences.

★ There is a wide range of specialist organisations which may be able to offer advice and information on the receiving environment.

★ The scale and duration of an intention are important in assessing magnitude of consequences.

★ Estimation of probabilities is difficult and it is always necessary to be very careful to define exactly what event is under consideration.

Chapter 4: Risk Assessment, Iterating the Process, and Risk Management

Risk estimation

4.1 For most intentions it is likely that more than one hazard will be identified. For each separate hazard, combining the probability of the consequences from Stage 4 and the magnitude of those consequences from Stage 5, as discussed in Chapter 3, yields an estimation of the risk. As already seen, both components are likely to be at best semi-quantitative; and it is not possible to propose a single formula for combining the two semi-quantitative estimates. Each component will represent a judgement on the basis of knowledge and experience and, in this respect, estimation of the risk is no different.

4.2 Despite these difficulties, a simple matrix can be useful as a focus for decision:

ESTIMATION OF RISK FROM CONSIDERATION OF MAGNITUDE OF CONSEQUENCES AND PROBABILITIES

	Consequences			
	Severe	Moderate	Mild	Negligible
Probability				
High	high	high	medium/low	Near zero
Medium	high	medium	low	Near zero
Low	high/medium	medium/low	low	Near zero
Negligible	high/medium/low	medium/low	low	Near zero

4.3 Such a matrix is a gross simplification which cannot represent the true complexity of the process referred to in paragraph 4.1 above: used with care it can be helpful but used uncritically the answers it appears to give could be misleading. In its application, such a matrix is unavoidably judgemental because the hazards must be evaluated on a case-by-case basis. For example, a particular case of "mild" consequences but "high" probability might be judged to be of "medium" or "low" risk. The decision should be on the basis of previous experience or relevant published information.

4.4   As noted in paragraph 4.1, it is likely that there will be more than one hazard. The overall risk will then be the combination of the risks arising from the individual hazards. Techniques exist for calculating the value of such combinations when they are quantitative and occur independently. Most environmental risk assessments are at best semi-quantitative however, and the person intending to carry out the operation must judge, on the merits of the particular case, how to combine the risks from each identified hazard. The logic that underlies the mathematical computation of combining risks, including consideration of whether the risks are additive or multiplicative, will apply equally to the combining of semi-quantitative and qualitative assessed risks. The difficulties are compounded in environmental risk assessment where the parts of the environment that potentially suffer harm are likely to be different for each hazard. Considerable personal judgement will be needed in making a sensible estimate of the risk. An important difficulty affecting the objectivity of anyone making a judgement is the effect of familiarity on perception of risk (discussed in paragraph 4.10 on).

Risk evaluation — a first look

4.5   The evaluation of the estimated risk is the second stage of risk assessment. It entails a judgement about how significant the estimated risk is. In economic theory, money is the universal yardstick against which environmental damage can be measured but, in practice, the difficulty is that of obtaining reliable and consistent valuations of intangible goods for which there is no direct market. This problem is tackled in "Policy Appraisal and the Environment"[1], which describes a number of techniques under the heading "Ways to value environmental resources".

4.6   One key factor in assessing the seriousness of the consequences is whether the environment is likely to be able to withstand the effects, i.e. whether sustainability is affected. The living environment is a dynamic process, which is constantly adapting to changes provoked as a result of human activity, or arising from natural causes such as variation in weather, earthquake activity, etc. To assess the magnitude of the outcome, it is necessary to consider whether the extent of the outcome exceeds normal environmental variations, and if it does, whether the

[1] *Policy Appraisal and the Environment*. Department of the Environment, HMSO, 1991. ISBN 0-11-752487-5.

effects might be nullified over time, that is, whether recovery is likely. Moreover, where there is uncertainty and potentially serious risks exist, precautionary action may be necessary.

4.7   According to the Royal Society report[2], evaluation is the process of determining the significance or value of the identified hazards and estimated risks to those concerned with or affected by the decision. It therefore includes the study of risk perception and the trade-off between perceived risks and perceived benefits. But perceptions of risk and benefit, and of the values of intangibles such as the quality of life will lead to different views on where to strike the balance between risks, costs and benefits which will vary from group to group.

4.8   Whilst the estimation of the damage arising from risks to the environment is difficult, nonetheless it is in some ways easier than evaluating those risks. Partly this is because knowledge and experience allow appropriate weighting to be given to the consequences and the probabilities of the realisation of hazards whereas risk evaluation involves making decisions based on what is a tolerable risk. Since Government, the public, industry, environmental groups, consumer groups etc often have different views about what constitutes a tolerable risk, risk evaluation by these different groups will usually produce different results.

4.9   A further difficulty is that the consequences and benefits may not fall on the same persons. These difficulties do not remove the need to evaluate the estimated risk but they should strongly affect who ought to make the judgements and decisions, if the evaluation is to be seen to be fair. This leads into the yet more subjective area of risk perception.

Risk perception

4.10   A different view to that in paragraph 4.7 above is that the perception of risk has nothing to do with its significance: the former is subjective whereas the latter is objective. However, that is an idealised view which does not correspond to the world as it is and how decisions are taken. This guide has already acknowledged that risk estimation and risk evaluation are subjective because the precise knowledge to be truly objective is rarely available. So it may well be right for decisions to be taken partly in response to pressures generated by perceptions of risk.

4.11   Sometimes those who have not studied the relevant statistics base their view on a significantly incorrect judgement of the probabilities and let this feed through to the risk assessment. Whilst it would be right for the decision maker not to be swayed by misjudgements of

[2] *Risk: Analysis, Perception and Management.* Royal Society, 1992. ISBN 0-85403-467-6

probability, it might still be necessary to explain the differences in perception and communicate the basis of decision to interested parties. This process would entail its own cost.

4.12   Other factors known to affect an individual's perception of risk include familiarity, control, proximity in space, proximity in time, fear of the unknown (the dread factor) and scale. These are discussed at greater length in Annex 5. Decision makers themselves need to guard against misperceptions arising from these causes and from over reliance on expert assessments, which can also be inaccurate because of the incompleteness of current knowledge.

Risk evaluation — further considerations

4.13   General confidence in the risk assessment and evaluation process is another factor to be considered. However open the process may be, those not directly involved or benefiting from the intention will suspect special pleading. It is one thing to check over a document for untruths but it is much harder to identify matters that have been entirely omitted. If, for example, an undertaking wished to present an operation as environmentally acceptable, it could easily conceal a hazard it wished not to be taken into account.

4.14   The appointment of independent expert assessors can help to solve this problem. For genetically modified organisms (GMOs) the Advisory Committee on Releases to the Environment (ACRE) fills such a role: it advises on all aspects of safety to humans and the environment arising from the release into the environment of new organisms. When such bodies are set up, it is important that they should be seen to be independent with no suspicion that they might act at the behest of a particular interest. Thereafter, such bodies must so conduct their business as to maintain public confidence. A particular danger that such bodies should guard against is "client capture", the phenomenon exemplified by the auditor who takes too much account of directors' view of a company's affairs and fails to protect the shareholder.

4.15   The evaluation of risk may change over time, as more information about the consequences and probabilities becomes available or better understood by those concerned. This points to the need to include alternative assumptions of the components of the risk evaluation in the overall assessment to see if the evaluation is sensitive to the assumptions. If it were, that would point to the need for caution.

4.16   The potential benefits of particular developments may outweigh the internal costs of extra environmental risks *ie* the costs borne by those who derive the benefits. This was the view held by some southern American countries in past decades in their approach to the destruction of the rainforest: for them, the immediate economic benefit was considered to outweigh environmental damage. There will be other similar situations in which immediate gains drive a decision even though there are indications of risk of damage to the environment: for example, DDT is still used in some countries afflicted by malaria. However, the concept of sustainability, because its effect is to attribute much higher values to long term environmental damage and to take account of external costs, should preclude the possibility of a series of short term judgements each of which sets short term gain above such damage. The international decision to curb the use of CFCs is an example of countries working for the common long term good despite the loss of shorter term benefits to themselves.

4.17   Increasingly, people are concerned not only by their standard of living but also by the quality of life. When decisions are made, most people want:

★ reassurance that "risky" operations are subject to appropriate regulatory or other control;

★ a green environment, with evident biodiversity, pleasant urban development with parks etc;

★ minimal pollution by chemicals, radioactive substances, noise, etc.

These elements of a good quality of life will tend to follow from the approach to risk assessment and risk management that is advocated in this guide. Together they contribute to a more sustainable development.

4.18   In evaluating risk, it may be important to consider whether environmental quality could be impaired as a result of a risk being realised. Environmental quality is important because it involves both scientific elements like biodiversity, and public perceptions of the "goodness" or "value" of the environment. One difficulty to date in this area has been the lack of objective measures of environmental quality that are based on nationally available biological data.

4.19   Progress towards the development of such indices of environmental quality is now being made. In the freshwater environment, the Institute of Freshwater Ecology has developed the River Invertebrates Prediction and Classification Scheme (RIVPACS)[3] for the National Rivers Authority. RIVPACS can be used to make statements about the biological quality of stretches of waterways. In the terrestrial environment, the Department of the Environment is supporting research into measures of

---

[3] *River Water Quality*. Ecological Issues Vol 1 British Ecology Society, 1990. ISBN 1-85153-850-X

environmental quality that will aid risk assessment and evaluation in relation to major industrial installations. The Department of the Environment's Countryside Information System[4] uses a combination of satellite image analysis and field survey to provide information about the extent and quality of major habitats in each one kilometre square of Great Britain. Predictions of habitat quality in particular locations are based on the average values for different types of land determined from a national sample survey carried out by the Institute of Terrestrial Ecology in 1990.

4.20   The decision to effect a benefit or gain environmentally in one respect may be at the expense of the environment in another. For example, the substitution of chemical pesticides by biological control agents leads to a reduced chemical loading on the soil, but it could, if not appropriately managed, mean that indigenous species are displaced. Any alternative approach should be subject to its own risk assessment and should not cloud the judgement to be made on the first approach. The fact that an alternative approach is worse than the one first tested does not mean that the first is acceptable.

4.21   Another potential area of difficulty is that of calling a halt to a process or trying to recall a substance or organism if, for example, monitoring showed that risks had been under-estimated. If, for practical purposes, an operation were unstoppable once begun, a substance could not be retrieved or did not decay to harmless products, or organisms did not die off, quite low risks might be considered unacceptable: these could all be considered examples of irreversible effects.

4.22   Risk evaluation and, at a later stage, risk management will usually fall to the person or authority responsible for making the decision. This may be a Government department, a regulatory authority, a business or an individual such as the production manager of a company. Whatever the position of the responsible person, all of the factors mentioned in this section on risk evaluation should be taken into account when evaluating the risk. The different components are likely to be weighted according to particular overall policies but it is usually prudent to reconsider the evaluation in the light of other perceptions to discover which are the important ones.

Iterating the process

4.23   A decision whether to go ahead with an intention should never be made on a single view of the components of the intention and of the

---

[4] The Countryside Information System (CIS) was developed for the Department of the Environment by the Terrestrial Ecology, Dart Computing and Nottingham University. CIS is available from the Software Sales Unit, Centre for Ecology and Hydrology, Maclean Building, Wallingford, Oxfordshire OX10 8BB.

costs and risks of fulfilling it. Rather, the whole process and even the intention itself should be refined in an iterative process which has three principal strands:

(i)   the refinement of engineering and technological design;

(ii) the consideration of non-monetary costs; and

(iii) the assessment of risk.

Some failures have resulted from not proceeding in this way.

4.24   The refinement of engineering and technological design is not the concern of this guide. The practitioners can be relied upon to exercise their competence. They will deliver their component of an intention in accordance with established safety standards and good practice and should achieve accepted standards of reliability at minimum cost by testing combinations of possibilities.

4.25   As mentioned in paragraph 2.1, consideration of non-monetary costs is not the concern of this guide but is dealt with in "Policy Appraisal and the Environment"[1].

4.26   After assessing the risk from each hazard and again after combining them into an overall risk assessment for the intention, it is necessary to answer the question:

Are the risks to human health and the environment from the intention intolerably high, or lower than some level judged to be acceptable, or falling into a tolerable region between these levels?

Posing this question in relation to risks arising from separate hazards and the combination of hazards avoids the danger of a low risk in one respect masking an unduly high risk in another.

4.27   Risks arising from an intention cannot ever be reduced to zero, because every action will have some effect on the environment. The risks need to be considered alongside the costs, consequences and benefits in order to decide whether the risks are tolerable. A tolerable risk implies that further reduction in the risk can be achieved only at excessive incremental cost and that the benefits that accrue from incurring the risk are judged to outweigh the disbenefits. If, at the end of the risk assessment stage, the risk is not judged to be low enough to be tolerable, the intention should be modified, in whole or in part, so as to reduce the consequences and/or the probability, and the risk then reassessed.

---

[1] *Policy Appraisal and the Environment*. Department of the Environment, HMSO, 1991. ISBN 0-11-752487-5.

This process should be repeated at least until the risk is low enough to be tolerable but the legal or other requirements described in the section "Some overriding requirements" below may require risks to be reduced even lower. Whichever is the case, then is the time to decide whether the cost is low enough to make the intention worthwhile.

4.28   The converse to the process described in paragraph 4.27 above is to modify an intention with a lower than tolerable risk to one with a risk at a higher level, albeit at which it is still tolerable solely in terms of risk. The purpose would be to achieve savings in costs or increased benefits. However, when the risks are imposed, most people's starting point is that risks should be as low as reasonably achievable: in many cases the section on "Some overriding requirements" may apply.

4.29   In the iterative process of assessing risks, costs and benefits, the more radical the changes to the basic intention or means of realising it, the more radical the reassessment of risks will have to be. New options may bring new risks and the reassessment should not be a mere review of what had been considered earlier. One option that should always be tested is the "Do nothing" option which will have its own risks, costs and benefits.

4.30   The iterative nature of the process with its feedback loops is illustrated by Diagram 2 (at the end of this chapter). The feedback loops show how judgements and decisions made at various stages are taken into account in modifying intentions. The diagram includes the monitoring phase described in the next chapter.

Some overriding requirements

4.31   According to the circumstances, the law or policy may subject an intention to a requirement such as:

ALARA	As low as reasonably achievable
ALARP	As low as reasonably practicable
BATNEEC	Best available technique not entailing excessive cost;
BPEO	Best practicable environmental option
BPM	Best practicable means

4.32   None of these terms is exactly equivalent to another: generally they are used within a strict legal context with the consequence that the implication of the use of one rather than another needs to be considered carefully in each particular application. Case law has established, for example, that 'practicable' is a more severe test than 'reasonably practicable': it follows that BPM is a very severe criterion.
Comments on the other terms are given in paragraphs 4.33 to 4.38.

4.33   A risk that has been reduced to ALARP corresponds to the definition of tolerable risk given in paragraph 4.27. In judging whether ALARP applies, the Health and Safety Executive take the view that a factor of disproportion between cost of risk reduction measure and benefit in risk alleviated is appropriate: when the risk is high and uncertain the disproportion must be gross; and when the risk is low then the disproportion need be no more than in balance with the benefit.

4.34   The application of BATNEEC normally means that the additional costs of avoiding environmental damage are justified by the benefits. BATNEEC would not require the reduction of risk from "low" to "negligible" if that would involve using very expensive techniques. The term BATNEEC is itself open to interpretation: some argue that if a measure to lower risk would become available only after development of that measure but not at the time of consideration than it is not truly available and so is not required under BATNEEC although it would be under ALARP.

4.35   Importantly, the application of BATNEEC means that the estimation of the risk associated with a particular operation can also change over time because new techniques and technologies are likely to be developed, while the cost of existing techniques will vary. Such changes can give rise to another iteration of the whole risk assessment process.

4.36   The term BPEO is a term of policy guidance. It is the option which provides the most benefit or least damage to the environment as a whole, at an acceptable cost. BPEO as a concept was introduced with Integrated Pollution Control under Part I of the Environmental Protection Act 1990. Operators of prescribed industrial processes which produce releases to more than one medium must *inter alia* ensure that BATNEEC is used to minimise pollution to the environment as a whole, having regard to the Best Practicable Environmental Option. Again, an element of cost versus environmental benefit/risk is brought into play in deciding what process option constitutes BPEO.

4.37   The application of the precautionary principle in cases of uncertainty may entail higher costs having some analogy with paying an insurance premium. However, for some processes and waste products there may be no BATNEEC and the process may be intrinsically unacceptable.

Risk management

4.38   As defined in paragraph 1.11, risk management is the process of implementing decisions about tolerating or altering risks. It is principally for clarity of exposition that risk management is being presented after risk assessment but additionally risk managers are often different people to the risk estimators and often to the risk evaluators. In practice, a decision to <u>alter</u> risks restarts the risk assessment process with the result that risk management becomes part of the iterative cycle. Moreover, it may become obvious at any stage in the risk assessment process that a particular part of an intention needs to be modified for some aspect (for instance, too high a probability for a well characterised hazard) with the result that risk management is not restricted to restarting the iterative process but becomes an integral part of it.

4.39   A risk management decision to <u>tolerate</u> a risk might be conditional on appropriate monitoring and, as a possible separate function, and control of the risk. The Nelson's column example of Chapter 1 suggested that one way of managing the risk was to monitor and maintain the column. Monitoring might consist of regular surveys of its verticality or inspection of the stonework. Controlling might be to take remedial or other action when a predetermined deviation from the vertical or the first evidence of spalling is observed. A corollary of the decision to monitor risk as part of risk management is that, if the appropriate action is not taken at the due time, the probability is increased that the hazard will be realised.

An example of a risk assessment

4.40   As previously mentioned an example of a risk assessment for the release of genetically modified wheat into the environment in a trial plot is described in Annex 2.

Summary

4.41   The principal points to note about risk assessment and risk management are set out below.

* Whilst risk estimation will always be judgmental, a matrix combining magnitudes and probabilities of consequences can be helpful.

* Sustainability is a key factor in risk evaluation.

* Risk perceptions depend on a wide variety of factors.

* Independent expert assessors can be a useful means of achieving objectivity.

* People are increasingly concerned with factors such as quality of life.

* The process of risk assessment and risk management is iterative.

* Irrespective of the risk assessment and cost benefit analysis, any intention may be subject to an overriding requirement such as ALARA.

* Risk management is inevitably part of the iterative process and should inform any monitoring system.

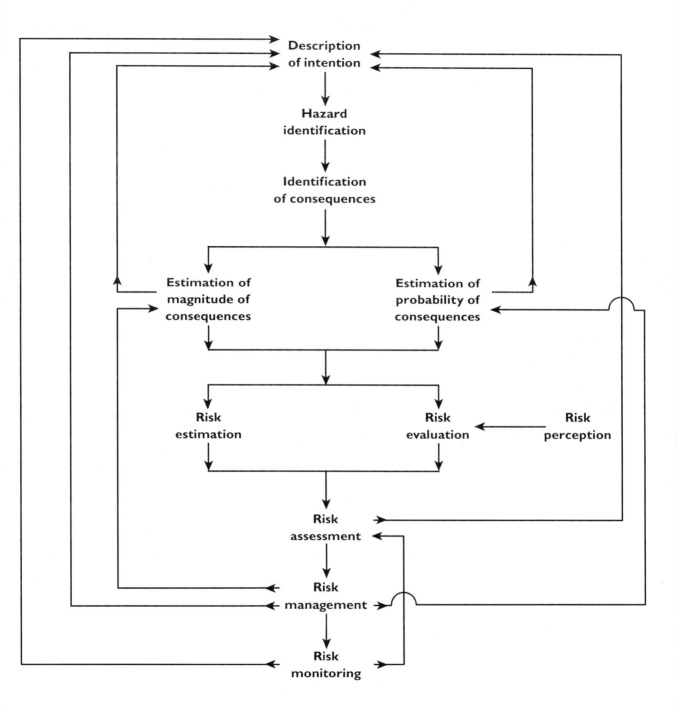

Diagram 2: From intention to risk management with feedback

Chapter 5: The Precautionary Principle and Sustainable Development

The sustainable development strategy

5.1   The UK Sustainable Development Strategy[1] argued that

"when potential damage to the environment is both uncertain and significant, it is necessary to act on the basis of the precautionary principle. This was described in the 1990 White Paper in the following terms:

'Where there are significant risks of damage to the environment the Government will be prepared to take precautionary action to limit the use of potentially dangerous materials or the spread of potentially dangerous pollutants, even where scientific knowledge is not conclusive, if the likely balance of costs and benefits justifies it.'"

5.2   It is easy to see why the precautionary principle (its origins are described in Annex 7) plays an important role in sustainable development. First 'prevention' often proves to use less resources than 'cure'. The precautionary principle is a prudent strategy under these conditions. Second a failure to take preventative action may result in long term damage that is too expensive to put right later. For example, simple measures can prevent the soil of an industrial site becoming contaminated. If these are not taken as a precaution, the site may become derelict at the end of its life because it is too expensive to decontaminate to allow it to be put to a new use. Natural capital that should have been passed on to later generations will thus have been eroded.

The precautionary principle and sustainable development

5.3   How does the precautionary principle fit into risk assessment? For the risk assessment of what befalls if the principle is disregarded, it is necessary first to identify the relevant *intention*. It is most useful to start with the alternative approach — a strategy that continues to expose a hazard to the environment until conclusive proof of harm presents itself. With this strategy, if conclusive evidence of harm were to be found later, then action would be taken immediately to reduce the exposure of the hazard and repair the damage. This would be the correct

---

[1] *Sustainable Development. The UK Strategy.* Cm 2426, HMSO, 1994. ISBN 0-10-124262-X

risk management strategy only if the risk assessment showed that its cost was no greater than a strategy with an early precautionary reduction of exposure.

Where the principle may not apply

5.4   An example of where the principle may not apply is that of some reactive air pollutants which have very short lifetimes in the atmosphere. As a consequence, if their emissions are reduced, ambient concentrations fall immediately. These pollutants may have clear harmful effects at high concentrations, but at normal ambient concentrations the available data may not be sufficient to show whether effects are still occurring. Suppose also that the understanding of the effects at higher concentrations suggests that any harmful effects are instantaneous, with complete recovery by the environment on removal of the pollutant. In such circumstances, the risk assessment shows that a strategy of continued emissions with associated environmental monitoring incurs no additional risk over a more precautionary strategy. It may even offer some gains on balance, since occasionally new evidence may emerge of a lower no-effect threshold which is safely above current atmospheric concentrations.

Where the principle could apply

5.5   It is also often the case that later clean-up is more expensive than early control of the hazard. In such a case delaying action until conclusive proof emerges poses the risk of wasting substantial resources compared with action under the precautionary principle. A high clean-up cost in a risk assessment may arise from either the nature of the damage caused or the fate of the pollutant in the atmosphere. Some examples are:

Heavy Metals. Heavy metals discharged into the atmosphere accumulate in soils and sediments. Thus when the source of discharge is terminated because of identified ecotoxic effects from heavy metals, the environmental concentrations may remain elevated for a very long time, with continued damage.

CFCs. Chlorofluorocarbons are very stable compounds which once released accumulate in the atmosphere. First signs of damage from CFCs to the stratosphere were detected in 1984 and have been the target of concerted international action since. However, because of the long atmospheric lifetime of CFCs, it is not expected that the stratosphere will show the first signs of repair until after the year 2000.

Dioxins. Dioxins are very stable chlorinated organic compounds formed in combustion processes such as waste incineration. They degrade very slowly and preferentially accumulate in the environment in animal fat and animal products like milk. Once in the environment, they are recycled through the food chain. Even if all inputs of dioxins to the environment were halted, it might be decades before levels fell significantly.

Acid Rain Damage. If rain is acidified above the level that can be neutralised by soil minerals from natural weathering, metal cations will go into solution and contaminate surface waters. Even when action is taken to reduce the acidification of rain it may take many decades for the soils to recover through natural mineralisation.

Radioactive waste. Some radioactive substances have half lives running into thousands of years. Once produced they are prohibitively expensive to transform to shorter lifetime material.

5.6   These examples show that when identifying hazards and analysing consequences, it is always important to identify the remaining lifetime of the hazard once action is taken to reduce its exposure, and to check the possibility that its consequences could accumulate in the environment. The realisation of some hazards may risk irreversible consequences. Hazards with long environmental lifetimes, accumulative or irreversible consequences, or with very wide spread distribution lead to the application of the precautionary principle when there is considerable uncertainty as to the link between the hazard and the consequence.

The precautionary principle and innovation

5.7   A particular case of the need to apply the precautionary principle arises from the risk assessment of new products or processes. Suppose that the hazards presented by a new product do not have a long environmental lifetime, and that the possible consequences of realising the hazard are not bio-accumulative. If conclusive evidence later emerges for these postulated consequences, it may still take some while to reduce exposure of the hazard. This reflects the difficulty of withdrawing the product from the market place. For example, halons have become such a standard chemical for fire extinguishing purposes that other competing technologies, such as fine water mists, have not been developed in parallel. As a consequence, the international programme for the phase-out of halons has been delayed in comparison with CFCs, with consequent continuation of damage from halons to the stratospheric ozone layer. The risk assessment of releasing onto a market place a new substance or compound with uncertain consequences should therefore take into account the risk that at some later point it might need to be withdrawn for reasons that, at the time of the assessment, are unforeseeable. In some cases this may justify the application of the precautionary principle. A good example is the possible introduction of a genetically modified organism: once released to the environment, it could never be recalled.

Using available scientific evidence

5.8   The precautionary principle is not a license to invent hypothetical consequences. Taking a risk assessment approach to the precautionary principle ensures that best use is made of what scientific evidence is available. In undertaking the risk assessment, it is necessary to pay careful attention to estimating the risks of harm that are consistent with the limited scientific evidence available.

5.9   In any risk assessment, it is important not to confuse 'no evidence of an effect' with 'evidence of no effect'. 'No evidence' may simply have indicated that, with the statistical tools to hand, insufficient statistical data has been accumulated to eliminate the effects of other randomly occurring disturbances. The effect is present but the analytic tools are too insensitive to detect it. It will therefore be necessary to look carefully at the available data to determine the largest level of harmful effect that could have been present while still failing to pass the statistical test employed.

5.10   Scientific evidence is seldom likely to be conclusive in respect to environment and health. The evidence is often deduced from animal studies and therefore only indirectly relevant to human health. With this in mind, health standards often introduce safety factors below the no effect level deduced from animal studies or other limited data to allow a degree of precaution. The preexistence of this safety factor should be recognised in any risk assessment.

5.11   In general, it cannot be legitimate to postulate a consequence of realising a hazard without at least one physical mechanism linking the hazard to the proposed consequence. For example, it is possible from health records to look for correlations between rare diseases and ambient contaminants. However, a correlation in the absence of any proposed mechanism by which the contaminant might have caused the disease makes it impossible to assume that the correlation reflects cause and effect. It could simply reflect an association through a common cause. Epidemiological evidence of this nature should indicate a risk assessment strategy of close exposure monitoring and focus the search for possible mechanisms.

A "green" interpretation

5.12   Organisations such as Greenpeace take a more radical interpretation of the precautionary principle and its application than the one described in paragraphs 5.1 to 5.11. They argue that the principle embraces the idea of avoiding the creation of new risks, on the general basis that this is not justifiable by need. One difficulty is that this would stifle innovation. They would further say that any exposition of the precautionary principle should include good husbandry. The need for good husbandry is not in dispute but it is fully covered in the concept of sustainable development as defined in the very first paragraph of this guide. It has therefore not been elaborated in this chapter.

Summary

★ The precautionary principle is important because 'prevention' often uses less resources than 'cure' and a failure to take preventative action may result in long term damage that is just too expensive to put right later.

★ A strategy of exposing a hazard to the environment until conclusive proof of harm would be correct only if its cost was no greater than a strategy with an early precautionary reduction of exposure.

★ The principle may not apply if, for instance, the risk assessment shows that with environmental monitoring the intention incurs no additional risk over a more precautionary strategy.

★ The principle applies for hazards with long environmental lifetimes or accumulative or irreversible consequences when there is considerable uncertainty as to the link between the hazard and the consequence.

★ The possibility that a new substance or compound with uncertain consequences might later need to be withdrawn should be taken into account in the risk assessment of releasing it onto a market.

★ The precautionary principle is not a license to invent hypothetical consequences. It cannot be legitimate to postulate a consequence of realising a hazard without at least one physical mechanism linking the hazard to that consequence.

★ Scientific evidence is seldom likely to be conclusive in respect to environment and health.

Chapter 6: Monitoring

Definition and purpose

6.1   Monitoring for the purposes of this guide is the systematic observation and measurement of physical, chemical or biological systems in order to establish their characteristics and changes over a period of time. Long term monitoring is monitoring for a period of over three years and is the norm for environmental monitoring, owing to the inherent variability of natural systems. These definitions are based in those in a Department of the Environment Guidance Note[1] which lists three reasons for long term monitoring:

   i)   because of <u>obligations</u> — statutory, regulatory and others, including commitments to international agreements;

   ii)   as an <u>alert mechanism</u> to record what is happening in order to determine when a situation has been reached which requires action; and

   iii) as a science <u>research facility</u> to provide long term time series baseline data for a wide range of research purposes.

This guide is not concerned with the first purpose.

6.2   The Guidance Note[1] also gives general advice on establishing a monitoring system.

The benefits of monitoring

6.3   The aim of monitoring is to achieve the continuous or periodic control of an operation, or to gain continuous or periodic information about certain aspects of the operation. In the former case, the monitoring constitutes part of the risk management techniques and is particularly associated with processes and operations (when it is usually short term or instaneous) but, in the latter, it represents the way in which:

   ★   the outcome of the risk assessment carried out prior to the operation is, or is not, confirmed; and

---

[1] *Long Term Monitoring. Science and Technology Guidance Note: 1/92.* Department of the Environment, 1992

★ information relevant to future risk assessments for similar operations can be obtained.

Process and operational monitoring for control is a well documented subject and will not be dealt with in this guide.

6.4   Monitoring is an expensive business but it can have many benefits. A carefully structured programme of environmental monitoring will provide a continuous loop between intentions and their outcomes. This will help to show not only what has been done wrong but what has been done right. In addition, monitoring will help reduce uncertainty about the environmental and ecological consequences of actions. However, the design and use of such monitoring schemes is in its infancy so the amount of practical detail that can be given is limited.

6.5   Monitoring actual outcomes of environmental effects is possible only in certain circumstances and interpreting the results in a meaningful way is possible only in a still more limited set of circumstances. Two particular difficulties are those of repeatability and control experiments (which are the common means of giving confidence in the results of a test). The difficulties arise because there is only a probabilistic connection between cause and effect: if the assessed probability is low, no effect would be expected but if one is unexpectedly observed, it may not be possible to retrieve the situation.

6.6   A further difficulty with many environmental effects is that they are not immediate or are not immediately manifest and their magnitude may be be attenuated or increased with the passage of time. An example is the delay factor in nitrates reaching aquifers after intense ploughing of grasslands and use of artificial fertilisers on chalk and sandstone areas. Another example is carcinogenicity, which is both time and concentration dependent.

6.7   For the longer term, although it may be difficult to rank different environmental risks, some effort to do so is necessary if risk management is to improve. There is a clear difference between the level of risk from, for instance, grime and noise and that from persistent pesticides but there may be no such clear distinction between, say, the use of different sorts of pesticides. By using the results of monitoring, the scale and complexity of techniques and processes can be developed in such a way that environmental harm is minimised. This has been the basis of the step-by-step approach which has been taken to the release of genetically modified organisms. The results of the first releases were fed into the risk assessment of larger scale and/or similar releases.

The design of an environmental monitoring programme

6.8   A prerequisite for the design of an effective environmental monitoring programme is a good understanding of the local ecosystem and the possible effects of the intention. This is because:

(i)   that understanding underlies the identification of the possible risks of the intention;

(ii)   monitoring is concerned with the change or lack of it in the receiving environment; and

(iii)   for cost-effectiveness, the monitoring system must be tailored to the affected environment.

Of these, (i) has been dealt with in Chapter 3.

6.9   In regard to (ii), monitoring of the effects of a new activity is only useful if there are baseline data to compare the monitoring data with. Many apparent effects can be the result of previous or nearby activities, or of natural phenomena with their inherent variability.

6.10   In order to be effective, monitoring should be targeted to where the most useful environmental information can be gained and should be performed with sufficient frequency that trends can be identified accurately. The cost of monitoring is an expense which should be taken into account in the overall costs of an intention: there is no point in monitoring effects that are not significant or incurring excessive cost by doing it too often or, conversely, so infrequently that the remedial of mitigating action that monitoring was intended to trigger is prompted too late to be effective.

6.11   For both (ii) and (iii) of paragraph 6.8, it is important to know clearly what you are looking for. Even so, the old adage will apply: expect the unexpected. The environment is so complex that there may be unexpected changes, so those charged with monitoring must be alert to pick up such changes and ensure their significance is properly assessed.

Chemical inputs

6.12   If risks of discharges to air or water are identified, then analyses of air or water samples should be undertaken. It is important to take as many samples as may be necessary to be statistically sure that the measured concentrations are representative of what is actually occurring in the environment. This may require expert advice. Samples should be taken upwind and downwind, or upstream and downstream of an activity in order to gain an idea of a before and after discharge effect.

6.13   It is important to monitor the biota in addition to the chemical component in the environment. There may be an unforeseen substance in the discharge that has not been detected in the analysis but has an effect on the organisms in the receiving environment or substances in combination may give rise to unforeseen effects.

Biological monitoring

6.14   Most ecosystems, terrestrial, aquatic or marine, consist of complex interactions of organisms with each other and the abiotic environment they occupy. Most habitat types are understood on a basic level but the detailed complexities of species interactions are not fully understood. Thus, it is unrealistic to attempt to monitor the fluctuations of every species. It is more useful to select key or "indicator" species and monitor these. The selection of these key species depends on the nature of the habitat which may be affected by the proposed activity.

Indicator species

6.15   An indicator species should have the following characteristics:

(i) be representative of the habitat under observation. If it is a visitor eg: migrating birds, it should be known to be a regular visitor. If there is a good local record of migrating birds, these can serve as an indicator because significant disturbance or decline in food sources will reduce the numbers nesting and breeding.

(ii) be sensitive to changes in the environment; it is necessary to have some knowledge of the parameters for survival eg water quality, acid concentrations etc. Lichens are effective indicators for industrial air pollution; salmonid fish require water containing few pollutants and relatively high levels of dissolved oxygen.

(iii) be readily identifiable and readily located to aid effective and accurate monitoring.

6.16   It is important to know the annual cycles and stages of the chosen indicator species. Many insect species, for example, will overwinter as larvae buffered in the soil or cold-hardy pupae or eggs, emerging as more active adult forms in spring and summer.

6.17   Changes in the population dynamics of one species will have knock-on effects and cause changes in other systems. For example, if the number of individuals of a plant species starts to decline, then so will the number of species associated with it, such as insects: the English Oak, for example, has approximately 240 species of insects associated with it.

6.18   Species such as predatory insects may not make accurate indicator species because their population numbers will depend on available prey species which may naturally fluctuate. Annual species of plants will have specific requirements for nutrients and moisture; if they fail to germinate, this could be due to natural prevailing environmental conditions such as drought or waterlogged soil, drainage or competition by other species that have colonised as a result of site disturbance or contamination. By contrast, plants or lichens make better indicator species because, in longer lived species, they occupy a fixed location and are easier to identify.

6.19   If the habitat contains rare or endangered species then ensuring their survival is likely of itself to be sufficient reason to monitor them directly. In addition, knowledge of other factors is important, for example, specific prey species and other food sources (plants, pollen), nesting or egg laying sites, and predators that could affect the population. Species are often rare or endangered <u>because</u> they are sensitive to environmental change and are often easily identified as a result of their rarity.

6.20   The Natural Environment Research Council (NERC)'s Unit of Comparative Plant Ecology (UCPE) runs the Integrated Screening Programme with other NERC institutes and other bodies. The UCPE (see Annex 6) can act as a useful source of reference for the response of species and function types to soil, air and water toxins. The UCPE can also set its measurements into the context of environmental variables not usually thought of as toxins.

Frequency of monitoring

6.21   Frequency of monitoring will depend on the nature of the activity; for example, the initial construction phase of a project often causes significant disturbance to nearby sites of environmental importance and regular monitoring might be necessary then.

6.22   If discharges of substances are a result of an activity, then the monitoring should be timed to coincide with the discharges to ensure they do not exceed prescribed amounts, in addition to longer term samples or even continuous monitoring to ensure that there are no unplanned discharges and to ascertain whether the substances are persisting in the receiving environment.

6.23   When monitoring the biota of an ecosystem, activity should be focused on when the species are most active, or at a sensitive stage of development. For example, migratory species will only appear seasonally, so this may require an intensive short period of activity. It is however, important to monitor the condition of the visitors' breeding sites in addition to relying on the presence of the species themselves. A decline in reproductive rates because the sites were adversely affected may not be identified until the next year when fewer individuals return. It is also important to monitor population structure, that is how many older individuals there are compared to young. A high old:young ratio indicates poor breeding success and may foreshadow a population collapse.

Sub-lethal effects

6.24   Although species may appear alive and well, they may be suffering sub-lethal effects which may eventually lead to mortality and population decline. This is a characteristic of long term exposure to polluting chemicals.

6.25   Sub-lethal effects may include stunted growth, reduced reproductive potential, morphological abnormalities (eg those imposed in molluscs as a result of tributyltin oxide contamination), increased susceptibility to disease as a result of other environmental stresses and reduced longevity. These can be detected more easily in established organisms such as long living plants or fish, but they are more difficult to detect in invertebrate populations. If such effects are observed, then further studies such as analysis of eggs, seeds, pollen etc will be necessary to establish the cause (which may be extraneous to the operation) and to assess reproductive potential and species recovery.

Responses to adverse effects

6.26   If the monitoring programme starts to identify adverse effects in the population dynamics of species, prompt and early action to correct these will be required. Such action, including its timing, should be specified in the scheme of risk management. Once that action has been taken the speed of recovery of the ecosystem will depend on the nature of the disturbance. In natural ecosystems there will often be a delay before the effects of an activity are manifested by the actual absence or noticeable death of species. Similarly, the correct and prompt response to observed adverse effects will not result in an immediate improvement in the quality of the affected ecosystem; there will be a delay before the ecosystem recovers.

Summary

- ★ Monitoring will reduce uncertainty about the environmental consequences of actions.

- ★ The monitoring system should be tailored to the affected environment.

- ★ Monitoring should be targeted to maximise its effectiveness, in terms of the intention to be monitored and the means of doing so.

- ★ Well chosen indicator species may be a useful form of monitoring.

- ★ Sub-lethal effects may be an early indicator of population decline.

- ★ When monitoring indicates the existence of conditions specified as requiring action in accordance with the risk management system, the response should be prompt.

Chapter 7: Summary and Conclusions

Summary and conclusions

7.1 Despite the difficulties in assessing the potential consequences of environmental risks, considerable value attaches even to describing an intention and identifying the hazards.

7.2 Describing the intention and how it is to be fulfilled and setting that intention in the before and after situations will help to ensure that the identification of hazards is tuned to the nature of the intention. To assist in assessing the impact on the environment, there is a wide range of specialist organisations which may be able to offer advice and information on the receiving environment. The combination of hazard and the relevant characteristics of the receiving environment will then lead to the identification of consequences so that, at the end of the process of risk assessment and risk management, a prognosis of an outcome provides the basis for monitoring and control.

7.3 The use of a structured approach to environmental risk assessment, applying, wherever possible, criteria for environmental harm, is a necessary but not in itself sufficient part of providing a sound basis on which decisions about particular actions can be made. Within a structured approach, at every stage, assumptions should be made explicit and recorded. Recording the analysis facilitates a reappraisal in changed circumstances or the light of new knowledge and enables others to recense the analysis.

7.4 Using a structured approach has a number of advantages. Firstly, by breaking down a problem of judgement into smaller parts, the resulting more detailed analysis may facilitate a judgement and allow a more quantified judgement to be made. Secondly, as the obverse to the first advantage, by revealing those matters on which it is not possible to make a judgement, analysis may indicate where more information should be sought. Thirdly, a structured approach may reveal areas of uncertainty and, whilst there is no general solution to the problem of uncertainty, its identification, if associated with significant potential damage, may indicate the need to invoke the precautionary principle. Fourthly, in new areas, analysis may indicate where regulatory measures are needed, if more market oriented approaches would not be effective.

7.5 The precautionary principle is important because 'prevention' often uses less resources than 'cure' and a failure to take preventative action may result in long term damage that is impossible or just too expensive to put right later. The principle applies for hazards with long environmental lifetimes or accumulative or irreversible consequences when there is considerable uncertainty as to the link between the hazard and the consequence. However, the precautionary principle is not a license to invent hypothetical consequences and should not be invoked in order to avoid making proper judgements.

7.6 In considering the two components of risk estimation - probability and magnitude of the consequences - it has been recognised that probabilities are difficult to judge and it is necessary to be very careful to define exactly what event is under consideration. When it comes to magnitudes, if the magnitude of a consequence cannot be estimated directly, it should be inferred from comparable precedents. In assessing magnitude of consequences, loss of species and functions is of prime significance and the scale and duration of an intention also are important. Whilst the process of combining magnitudes and probabilities of consequences into a risk estimation will always be judgmental, a matrix can be helpful.

7.7 Sustainability is a key factor in risk evaluation, which like risk estimation is very judgmental. Among the factors affecting judgement is that of risk perception. Risk perceptions vary with point of view and a wide variety of factors, such as familiarity and degree of control, affect the subjective assessment of risk. Moreover, people are increasingly concerned with factors such as quality of life. The appointment of independent expert assessors can be a useful means of overcoming some of these problems of perception and evaluation and of achieving and demonstrating objectivity.

7.8 Risk assessment will lead on to risk management decisions that will reflect priorities that have been assigned to various parameters and components, including the less tangible factors mentioned in paragraph 7.7 Making decisions on the basis of risk assessment will contribute significantly to achieving sustainable development. However, irrespective of the risk assessment and cost benefit analysis, some intentions may be subject to an overriding requirement such as ALARA which preempts other judgements.

7.9   The whole process of risk assessment and risk management is iterative in two ways: as a process for any particular intention; and in wider terms in that, through monitoring systems, as information is gathered from current operations, successive risk assessments and risk management can draw on the broader knowledge and deeper understanding from an increasing bank of experience. Thus, over time, the results of a structured approach to the assessment and management of risk, can help substantially in making decisions and setting policies.

7.10   Risk management and monitoring go hand in hand. The monitoring system should be tailored to the affected environment. A good monitoring system will reduce uncertainty about the environmental consequences of actions. However, it is important that when monitoring indicates the existence of conditions specified as requiring action in accordance with the risk management system, the response should be prompt.

7.11   To maximise its effectiveness, monitoring should be targeted in terms of the intention to be monitored and the means of doing so. For these purposes, well chosen indicator species may be a useful form of monitoring.

Envoy

7.12   Risk assessment and risk management in the context of sustainable development is still in its infancy. As with all new developments, it is often treated with some scepticism and sometimes dismissed as being too difficult. It is only by trying to deal with the undoubted difficulties that they will be overcome, slowly at first but with gathering speed as the feedback from monitoring improves knowledge and as demonstrated results win over sceptics.

Annex 1: Abbreviations and glossary

Abbreviations

ACHS	Advisory Committee on Hazardous Substances
ACRE	Advisory Committee on Releases to the Environment
ALARA	as low as reasonably achievable
ALARP	as low as reasonably practicable
BATNEEC	best available techniques not entailing excessive cost
BPEO	best practicable environmental option
BPM	best practicable means
DOE	Department of the Environment
MAFF	Ministry of Agriculture, Fisheries and Food
NOEC	no observed effects concentration
PEC	predicted environmental concentration
RIVPACS	River Invertebrates Prediction and Classification Scheme

Glossary

Consequences	adverse effects or harm which cause the quality of human health or the environment to be impaired in the short or longer term.
Exposure (normally refers to external exposure)	the amount of substance ingested, the amount in contact with the skin or either the amount inhaled or the concentration in the atmosphere (as appropriate).
Exposure-response curve	the mathematical or graphical representation of the link between exposure and response or effect.
Hazard	a property or situation that in particular circumstances could lead to harm.

Intention	includes the manufacture and use of a substance; the creation, testing and release of an organism; the construction or demolition of some artifact or scheme; an operation or process; any combination of intentions: and, for all intentions, taking account of inputs, useful and waste products, by-products and emissions.
Probability	is the mathematical expression of chance (for instance, 0.20, equivalent to a 20 per cent or a one in five chance), wherever this usage is possible but in many cases it can be no more than a prospect which can be expressed only qualitatively. The definition applies to the occurrence of a particular event in a given period of time or as one among a number of possible events.
Risk:	a combination of the probability, or frequency, of occurrence of a defined hazard and the magnitude of the consequences of the occurrence.
Risk assessment	consists of **risk estimation** and **risk evaluation**. This definition of risk assessment, by incorporating risk evaluation, goes beyond that on the EC Directive relating to new substances.
Risk estimation	is concerned with the outcome or consequences of an intention taking account of the probability of occurrence.
Risk evaluation	is concerned with determining the significance of the estimated risks for those affected: it therefore includes the element of risk perception.
Risk management	is the process of implementing decisions about accepting or altering risks.
Risk perception	is the overall view of risk held by a person or group and includes both feeling and judgement.
Sustainable development	is development that meets the needs of the present without compromising the ability of future generations to meet their own needs.

Appendix I to Annex I

Definitions in EC Council Directive 93/67/EEC

(a) 'hazard identification' is the identification of the adverse effects which a substance has an inherent capacity to cause;

(b) 'dose (concentration) - response (effect) assessment' is the estimation of the relationship between dose, or level of exposure to a substance, and the incidence and severity of an effect;

(c) 'exposure assessment' is the determination of the emissions, pathways and rates of movement of a substance and its transformation or degradation in order to estimate the concentrations/doses to which human populations or environmental compartments are or may be exposed;

(d) 'risk characterisation' is the estimation of the incidence and severity of the adverse effects likely to occur in a human population or environmental compartment due to actual or predicted exposure to a substance, and may include 'risk estimation', *i.e.,* the quantification of that likelihood;

(e) 'recommendations for risk reduction' is the recommendation of measures which would enable the risks for man and/or the environment in connection with the marketing of the substance to be lessened. They may include:

(i) modifications to the classification, packaging or labelling of the substance proposed by the notifier in the notification submitted in accordance with Article 7 (1), 8 (1), or 8 (2) of Directive 67/548/EEC;

(ii) modifications to the safety data sheet proposed by the notifier in the notification submitted in accordance with Article 7 (1), 8 (1) or 8 (2) of Directive 67/548/EEC;

(iii) modifications to the recommended methods and precautions or emergency measures, as set out in sections 2.3, 2.4 and 2.5 of Annex VIIA, VIIB or VIIC, proposed by the notifier in the technical dossier of the notification submitted in accordance with Article 7 (1), 8 (1) or 8 (2) of Directive 67/548/EEC;

(iv) advice to the relevant control authorities that they should consider appropriate measures for the protection of man and/or the environment from the risks identified.

Annex 2: Risk assessment for the release of genetically modified spring wheat

Note: This annex is drawn directly from an application for a consent to release genetically modified spring wheat submitted under the Genetically Modified Organisms (Deliberate Release) Regulations 1992.

The release is a small scale trial to assess the field performance of genetically modified (GM) spring wheat derived using different techniques of genetic modification. The trial is to evaluate the effectiveness of the inserted genes under field conditions.

The release consists of three different GM wheat lines with the following inserted genes for use as markers: a bacterial gene, technically known as the beta-glucuronidase gene, which gives rise to blue colouration of the plant for use in assays; a bacterial gene, technically known as the hydrofolate reductase gene, which gives rise to resistance to a chemical called methotrexate; and, a plant gene, technically known as the B-peru gene, which gives rise to red pigmentation of the seed coat.

The GM wheat seeds were sown in March 1994. The GM wheat was surrounded with border rows of non-GM wheat to restrict pollen flow. Monitoring was at weekly intervals during the release. Prior to full seed maturity, the seed was hand collected for analysis and the remaining plant material was disked and ploughed into the release site. After harvest, the release site was to be left fallow and monitored for two years. Any regrowth of wheat would be destroyed.

Summary: The environmental impact of the proposed trial is assessed as effectively equivalent to commonly grown wheat. This assessment is based on the data available to date. No risk could be identified relating to phenotypic and genetic instability, gene transfer, seed establishment and any pathogenicity of effect on non-target organisms.

I. HAZARD IDENTIFICATION

Recipient organism: the recipient organism is spring wheat *(Triticum aestivum)*. Spring wheat is grown in the UK as an agricultural crop. The crop is managed within the agricultural environment and does not present a hazard. It is not known to be invasive and to colonize natural environments.

Donor organisms: the donor organisms for the introduced DNA sequences are maize and the bacterium *Escherichia coli*. Maize is a commonly grown agricultural crop worldwide. *Escherichia coli* is an ubiquitous enterobacterium, not normally pathogenic. The genes transferred from these donors to spring wheat are used as marker genes.

The modified organism: the products of the introduced genes have not been reported to be toxic. They will not give any selective advantage to the modified wheat. Two of the three lines proposed for the test have presented a partial male sterility when grown in the greenhouse.

Potential events

i. **Potential for transfer of genetic material between the modified wheat and other organisms**

- transfer of genes to other wheat plants by pollen;

- transfer of genes to representatives of the genus *Agropyron* and *Secale*, which may be cross-compatible under certain conditions: weediness or invasiveness of the produced hybrids;

- horizontal transfer of genes to microorganisms or other plants.

ii. **Phenotypic and genetic instability**

- any change of the insertion site or any change occurring in the insertion.

iii. **Pathogenicity**

- none.

iv. **Potential for survival, establishment and dissemination**

- the modified wheat as a weed (survival and establishment);

- dissemination of seeds.

v. **Other negative effects on organisms (non-target organisms)**

- consumption of modified wheat plants or their seeds by birds or rodents.

II. ENVIRONMENTAL EXPOSURE ASSESSMENT

The proposed field test with modified spring wheat is a small scale test [less than 40m², including the border rows of non transgenic wheat]. It will take place within an agricultural environment where wheat is regularly grown. Standard agricultural practices for breeding, including a net and a fence, will be used.

Wheat and cross-compatible relatives: the nearest wheat field will be located at more than 500m. The distance is far superior to the largest isolation distance advised for the production of basic and pre-basic seeds (50m). Intergeneric hybrids between hexaploid wheat and six genera have been reported. Only representatives of the genera *Agropyron* and *Secale* are present in the UK. *Agropyron repens* is a major weed of wheat and may be present in the vicinity of the test plot. *Secale cerealis* will not be present within at least 1 km from the trial site.

Target organisms: there is no target organism because the introduced genes are marker genes.

Others: from the location and type of release, there will be no effects on water, soil or air; and hazards related to these can be discounted.

III. RISK ASSESSMENT

i. Potential for transfer of genetic material between the modified wheat and other organisms

Probability of gene transfer to other wheat plants by pollen: wheat pollen is very heavy and falls on the style; its viability is very short, usually not more than 1 to 3 minutes. Wheat is self-fertilising to 99%. These characteristics of wheat pollen and the isolation of the plot from other wheat fields render the probability of gene transfer through pollen negligible. In addition, two of the proposed lines show a partial male sterility.

Probability of gene transfer to cross-compatible relatives by pollen: *Agropyron repens* might be present in the vicinity of the trial plot. Despite a considerable amount of work on *in vivo* hybridization of wheat x *Agropyron*, natural compatibility and the spontaneous production of hybrids able to survive and multiply in nature has never been reported. *Secale secalis* will not be present within 1 km of the trial site.

Consequence of gene transfer by pollen: the consequences of gene transfer to other wheat, *Agropyron* or *Secale* plants, if it occurs, would be negligible as the market genes introduced and their products will not change the behaviour of the plant in the field.

Therefore: the risk associated to
a transfer of the introduced genes to
other wheat plants or to cross-compatible
plants is assessed as: Effectively zero.

There is no documented evidence which could give us reason to expect that horizontal gene transfer from the modified wheat to other plants or to microorganisms will occur.

Therefore: the risk associated to an horizonal   Not known but
transfer of the introduced expected genes to   expected to be
other plants or to microorganisms is assessed as: effectively zero.

ii. Phenotypic and genetic instability

The observations and analyses carried out on plants from successive generations derived from the transformed plants showed a stability of the insertion. Specific effects resulting from tissue culture (e.g. somatoclonal variation) could be revealed under field conditions. Such genetic changes in the existing wheat genome would present no greater impact on the environment than wheat from mutation breeding processes.

Therefore: the risk associated to phenotypic
and genetic instability is assessed as: Effectively zero.

iii. Pathogenicity

No hazard regarding pathogenicity could be identified due to the nature of the donor organisms, the recipient plant and the genes transferred.

Therefore: the risk associated to
pathogenicity is assessed as: Effectively zero.

iv. Potential for survival, establishment and dissemination

Probability of survival: survival of wheat is by the formation of seeds. Seeds could remain in the soil if they do not germinate just after planting or if mature seeds or spikes fall on the ground. The experience gained at New Farm Crops shows that survival of spring wheat seeds in soil does not exceed 2 years. In the proposed trial, seeds will be harvested before full maturity. In addition, the site will be treated with an herbicide after harvest and monitored for regrowth during two years. Regrowth, if any, will be removed and incinerated. Therefore, any hazard from survival is only relevant if seeds are taken away from test plot (see below).

Probability of dissemination: dissemination of wheat seeds by birds and rodents is known and may occur. According to standard breeding practices, a net and a fence will be used to protect the trial. This will also minimize the probability that seeds could be carried away by animals. The small size of the plot, the limited duration of the trial and the early harvest of the grains will also greatly reduce total potential exposure.

Probability of establishment: the herbicide treatment and the monitoring of the plot will render the probability of establishment of transgenic wheat on the trial site negligible. Establishment of seeds carried away from the trial area is of low probability. Wheat seeds outside wheat fields are in competition with other plants and therefore rarely develop into a mature plant, setting seeds. Wheat has never been reported as a self sowing population in the UK.

Consequence of seed survival, dissemination and establishment: if seed survival, dissemination and establishment would occur, the consequence of this event would be "effectively zero". The products of the genes introduced are not expected to make the wheat seeds more persistent, easier to disseminate or to favour seed establishment.

Therefore: the risk associated to seed survival, establishment and dissemination is assessed as: Effectively zero.

v. Other negative effects on organisms (non-target organisms)

As stated previously, the probability that animals could come in contact with the seeds is low. The products of the genes have no reported toxicity. Therefore, the consumption of seeds is not expected to have any detrimental effects on animals.

Therefore: the risk associated to effects on non-target organisms is assessed as:

Not known but expected to be: effectively zero.

III. OVERALL RISK ASSESSMENT

The overall risk of damage to the environment is EFFECTIVELY ZERO as the following constituents of the risk have been assessed as:

Transfer by pollen to other wheat plants	Effectively zero
Transfer by pollen to cross-compatible species	Effectively zero
Horizontal transfer to plants and micro-organisms	Not known but expected to be effectively zero
Phenotypic and genetic instability	Effectively zero
Pathogenicity	Effectively zero
Seed survival	Effectively zero
Seed dissemination	Effectively zero
Seed establishment	Effectively zero
Effect on non-target organisms	Not known but expected to be effectively zero

The data available to date show that the genetically modified wheat plants behave like the non-modified wheat plants, apart from 1) the expression of the inserted genes and 2) a partial male sterility in two of the three proposed lines. A phenotypic and genetic instability was not observed up to now. The risk linked with gene transfer is assessed as effectively zero, due to the characteristics of wheat pollen and the isolation of the test site. The risk linked with survival, dissemination and establishment of seeds is also assessed as effectively zero as seed dissemination by birds and rodents, if it occurs, will have no detrimental consequence for the environment. Given the nature of the gene products, no pathogenicity or effects on non-target organisms can be identified.

Annex 3: Assessing the potential environmental risk for a household product: a simplified example

1.   A fabric washing formulation is a typical example of a household product containing some toxic components. For such a product, this annex illustrates the assessment of the potential risk to the aquatic environment of the principal toxic component, namely, the surface active agent or surfactant. In this illustration, the risk is treated in isolation: no account is taken of synergistic effects.

2.   After the washing process, water from a washing machine is normally discharged to the household drainage system, which in most cases then passes via a main sewer to the sewage treatment works, where purification takes place. The purified effluent from the works is then commonly discharged to a river.

3.   To estimate the magnitude of the consequences arising from this discharge of surfactant to the aquatic environment, we need to

(i)   identify the hazards, which are

- toxicity to aquatic organisms, and

- degradability of active agents (which is not dealt with in this annex); and

(ii)   estimate the environmental concentration, given by

- the information on the quantities discharged,

- the removal of the surfactant by sewage treatment, and

- the dilution afforded by the surface waters receiving the treated sewage works effluent.

4.   The likely environmental concentration of the surface active agent in effluents as they are discharged to surface waters can be predicted from the following data, applicable to the UK:

(i)   Surface active agent annual usage: 80,000 tonnes (industry data)

(ii) Percentage removal by sewage treatment: 98 (monitoring and experimental data)

(iii) Population of UK : 55 x 10^6

(iv) Average daily flow to sewage treatment: 200 l/hd (water industry data includes for population, inflow etc)

5.   Assuming discharges are spread over 365 days in the year, the concentration of unchanged surfactant in the effluent, the emission concentration, EC, is calculated from the expression:-

$$EC = \frac{(i) \times [100-(ii)]}{(iii) \times (iv) \times 100} = \frac{(80000 \times 10^{9)}) \times [100-98]}{(55 \times 10^6) \times (200 \times 365) \times 100}$$

= 0.4 mg/l (where, 10^9 converts tonnes to milligrams.)

Note that the assumption that discharges are spread uniformly over the 365 days of the year is explicit and the calculation could readily be refined by applying an estimated factor for the ratio of the peak concentration for a shorter period to the average concentration over a year.

6.   Since sewage effluents are normally discharged to a river, the second step is to take account of the dilution afforded to sewage effluent discharges. For modelling purposes, this dilution factor is assumed to be 10:1 (although in the UK the dilution factor is often greater than 10:1) thus giving a Predicted Environmental Concentration, PEC$_{local}$ of 0.04 mg/l. Again, the assumptions are explicit.

7.   To assess the consequences, the PEC$_{local}$ is compared with the effects data, ie the results of testing using for example fish, water flea and algae as the target organisms. The particular surfactants used in European washing powders when tested using the water flea as the test organism tend to result in a no observed effect concentration (NOEC) in long term tests of about 1 mg/l. The same order of NOEC has been found with fish.

8.   Since for practical reasons, the number of species tested is limited, a commonly used approach is to extrapolate the test results to cover whole ecosystems by the application of a safety assessment factor. The factor is also needed to take account of variations in sensitivity between species and, when appropriate, extrapolation between acute and chronic sensitivity. The assessment factors recommended for use in the characterisation of aquatic risk are given in the Technical Guidance

Document accompanying the European Commission Directive 93/67/EEC[1] on the evaluation of the potential risks of new notified substances. The guidance for this case would be to use a factor of 10 which is applied to the lowest value of the NOEC obtained from tests with fish, daphnia and algae.

9. The value of the NOEC for the most sensitive species tested is divided by the factor to give a Predicted No Effect Concentration, PNEC. This is not defined as a safe level, but rather one at which adverse effects are not expected to occur. In this example, it is assumed the water flea was the most sensitive species found in long term tests with a NOEC of 1 mg/l. Applying the recommended value of the safety assessment factor of 10 gives a <u>PNEC of 0.1 mg/l</u>. This means that any discharge greater than 0.1 mg/l could be expected to give rise to harmful effects to at least some aquatic organisms.

10. If the ratio of PEC_{local}:PNEC<1 then a substance is considered to be of no immediate concern *ie* the magnitude of the consequences is low or negligible. In the example PEC_{local} is <u>0.04 mg/l</u> and hence the ratio to PNEC is less than 1 by a factor of 2½. The predicted environmental concentration implicitly that the probability that the active agent will be present at that concentration is 1. Therefore the risk arising from the hazard of toxicity to aquatic organisms is low or effectively zero at the estimated market tonnage.

11. It is quite possible that the dilution available on discharge of the effluent from the sewage treatment plant may be considerably greater than that used in the model calculation. This factor may decrease further the value of the predicted environmental concentration and hence the ratio PEC:PNEC. The converse is possible due to a poorly operating sewage treatment works, higher use of the product in a particular area etc., and at some point the ratio could exceed 1 therefore giving rise for concern and the possible need to refine the estimation of PEC_{local} and hence the magnitude of the consequences.

12. It is interesting to note that the estimate of the environmental concentration is realistic since the actual concentration in rivers of the surface active agent considered is found to be in the range 0.01-0.1 mg/l.

---

[1] *EC Directive 93/67/EEC.* Official Journal of the European Communities, L227, 8 September 1993. HMSO

Annex 4: Some techniques for failure analysis

1. This annex illustrates by worked examples two techniques:

(i) for setting out the combination of circumstances that could lead to particular outcomes; and

(ii) for calculating the probability of the outcomes.

Both techniques use a diagram to demonstrate the logic of possible combinations of circumstances and of the calculation of the probabilities of the various outcomes (see figures 1 and 2 at end of annex). The first example is an "event tree" and the second is a "fault tree". Both are based on examples in the Health and Safety Commission's "Major hazard aspects of the transport of dangerous substances".[1]

Example 1. Event tree for liquified gas transfer spill.

2. Figure 1 illustrates the calculation of the probability of a number of different outcomes that could stem from a spill of liquified gas during the transfer of the gas from a cargo vessel to a terminal facility.

3. The possible events whose probabilities are analysed have been condensed into a simplified set of eight possibilities comprising: 20-, 10-, 5- or 2-minute full bore flows or 20-, 10-, 5- or 2-minute leaks.

4. The events depend on whether

(i) there is a ranging failure or a connection failure;

(ii) the operator is incapacitated;

(iii) the operator reacts immediately, defined as within one minute of the rupture; and

(iv) the emergency shut-down (ESD) system is effective;

---

[1] *Major hazard aspects of the transport of dangerous substances.* Health and Safety Commission, HMSO, 1991. ISBN 0-11-885676-6.

71

5.　The probabilities for each branch of the event tree are necessarily based on expert judgement. However, sensitivity tests have shown that uncertainty in the branch probabilities does not seriously affect the overall results.

6.　Referring again to Figure 1, it can be seen that it is built up logically from the left across to the results on the right. Various events are possible and whether they occur is answered by "Yes" or "No" (shown in the figure by an upward or downward branch respectively). Each answer has an effect on the outcome. Thus, the upper part of the figure leading to the top three results reflects the nature of a ranging failure in that

(i)　it always leads to a full bore spill but cannot lead to a 20 minute full bore spill;

(ii)　the potential result of a 10 minute full bore spill can be reduced to a 5 minute full bore spill provided the operator is not incapacitated; and, granted that proviso,

(iii)　the result will be reduced to a 2 minute spill if the ESD system is effective.

7.　The chain of events that is shown by highlighting in Figure 1 illustrates the case when

- the transfer spill is caused by a connection failure (0.94); and

- does not result in a full bore rupture (0.90).

- the operator is not incapacitated (0.97);

- the operator does react immediately (0.50); and

- the ESD is effective (0.90).

where the relevant probabilities are shown by the figures in brackets.

8.　This is the combination of requirements for achieving the least bad result of a 2-minute leak. The probability of that outcome is calculated by multiplying the independent probabilities together:

$$0.94 \times 0.90 \times 0.97 \times 0.50 \times 0.90 = 0.369$$

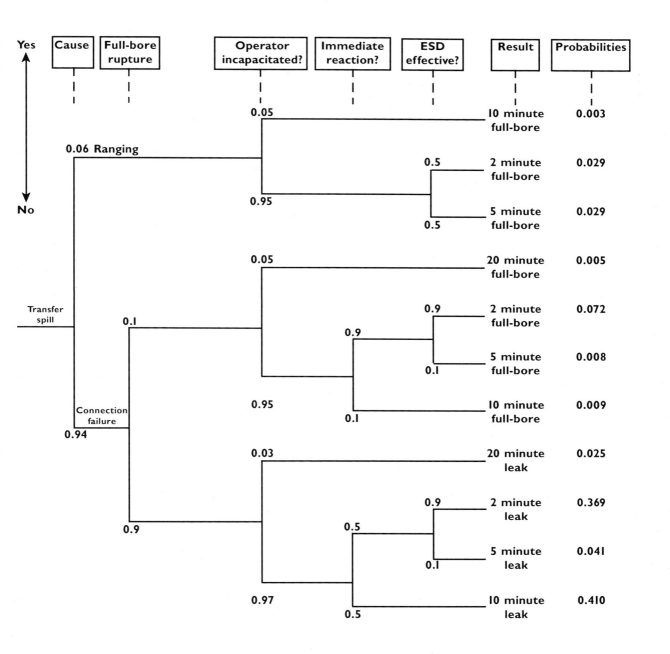

Figure 1: Example event tree for liquefied gas transfer spill

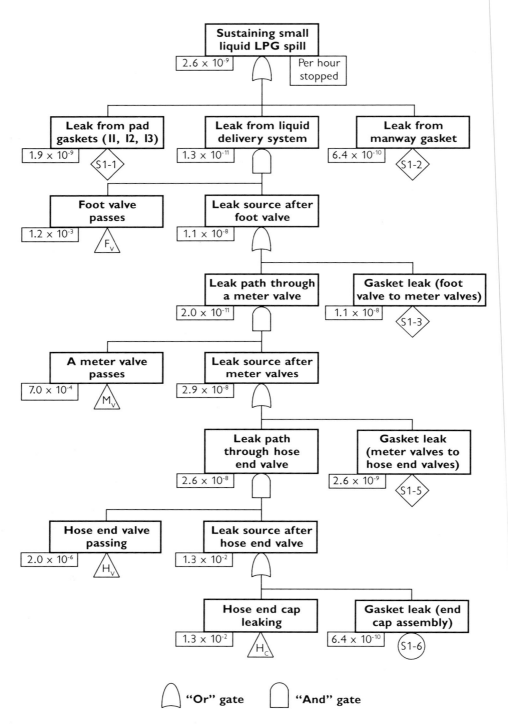

Figure 2: LPG road tanker small leak fault tree.
Leaks applicable to short term stops. Units: per hour stopped.

Example 2. Fault tree for a small leak from a liquified petroleum gas (LPG) tanker during short term stops.

9.   Figure 2 illustrates the calculation of the probability of a small leak from a Liquified Petroleum Gas (LPG) road tanker during short term stops. The probability is that of the occurrence of a sustained small leak and is calculated per hour that the road tanker is stopped.

10.   Figure 2 shows the various faults that could occur and which separately or in combination lead to a sustained small liquid LPG spill. The figure is no more than a systematic description of possible faults, set out so that the calculation proceeds from the bottom to the top. It shows how the various faults can or must combine before there is a spill. As with the first example, the probabilities assigned to each item of the fault tree are necessarily based on expert judgement. The diagram makes use of two symbols shown in the legend (the "Or" gate and the "And" gate) which can best be understood by those unfamiliar with the jargon by reference to the top part of the figure as explained in paragraphs 11 and 12 below.

11.   The second row of boxes deals with three possible causes of spills and shows their respective probabilities (given in brackets below):

- leak from pad gaskets (1.9×10^{-9});

- leak from liquid delivery system (1.3×10^{-11}, equivalent to 0.013×10^{-9}); and

- leak from manway gasket (6.4×10^{-10}, equivalent to 0.64×10^{-9}).

A leak from any of the three sources (pad gasket, liquid delivery system, or manway gasket) could lead to the sustained small liquid LPG leak shown in the topmost box and each is therefore linked to it by an "Or" gate. The probability of each separate cause combines additively to the overall probability of the final event. Thus,

$$1.9 \times 10^{-9} + 0.013 \times 10^{-9} + 0.64 \times 10^{-9} = 2.553 \times 10^{-9}$$

which, rounded, is the overall probability of 2.6×10^{-9} shown for a sustained small liquid LPG spill.

12.   The figure shows that before there can be a leak from the liquid delivery system (the central box in the second row) two conditions (shown in the third row) must occur in combination: those conditions are that there is a source of leak after (downstream) of the foot valve and that the foot valve is passing liquid. These two events are therefore shown linked to their consequence by an "And" gate. The probability

of each separate cause combines multiplicatively to the overall probability of the consequent event. Thus

$$1.1 \times 10^{-8} \times 1.2 \times 10^{-3} = 1.32 \times 10^{-11}$$

which, rounded, is the overall probability of 1.3×10^{-11} a leak from the liquid delivery system.

12.   Many of the faults and their associated probability of occurrence are themselves the result of a similar calculation. Thus a fault tree calculation would underlie the probability of occurrence of the faults associated with the three valves shown in boxes on the left of the figure.

Annex 5: Some factors affecting perceptions of risk

1.   There are a number of factors which are known to affect people's perception of risk: they include familiarity, control, proximity in space, proximity in time, the dread factor and scale.

Familiarity. People tend to underestimate the risks which are familiar to them and to overestimate those that are unfamiliar. Thus the practitioners of soccer and hang gliding have a fair idea of the risks they take but the general public underestimates the risks of an accident in soccer and overestimates the risks of one in hang gliding.

Control. People tend to underestimate the risks from an activity over which they have control compared to one in which they are in other people's hands. Despite published statistics on fatalities, driving a car is often considered to be safer than flying in an aeroplane. Moreover, people tend to demand greater protection from events over which they have no control.

Proximity in space. Although the risk per person in the population near to an activity may be greater than the the average risk in the population as a whole, people may overestimate the risks of something which might occur near to them and underestimate those that will occur at a location remote from them. This is one factor in the "Nimby" syndrome.

Proximity in time. People tend to ignore the effects of risks that are going to arise much later in time. Whilst discounting, in the economists's sense of reflecting time consequences, should be standard practice, it should not be duplicated by also taking less account of the risk itself.

The dread factor. People exaggerate the risks associated with phenomena they do not understand. Risks associated with machinery are under-regarded whilst those associated with, say, radiation are exaggerated. Moreover, people tend to demand greater protection from events which they do not understand.

The scale factor. The media are more concerned with one large scale consequence that a large number of individually smaller consequences which sum to a greater overall consequence. An obvious example is in car accidents where a pile-up causing 50 injuries is more newsworthy than 50 separate accidents each causing an injury. A consequence of the greater media attention to large scale accidents is that they concern politicians and businesses more.

2.   There is also some research evidence to show that the public view about the risk associated with a particular intention will depend principally on the consequences: the public will either largely ignore the probabilities or base their view on a significantly incorrect judgement of the probabilities. The expert tends to approach an assessment starting with the probabilities and let this feed through to the risk assessment. Whilst it would be right to ignore misperceptions of probability, it may still be necessary to explain the differences in perception to the public. This process may entail its own cost. It may also be necessary to recognise that there may be significant inaccuracies or lack of certainty in the risks assessed by the experts themselves.

3.   Risk policy should reflect the best objective analysis but in the short term, may have to modify the conclusions drawn from that analysis to take account of the perceptions of those who will be affected by the decision. In the longer term it may be possible to educate those affected to a more informed and less troubled perception of some risks. British Nuclear Fuels plc has undertaken a large scale exercise at its Sellafield site to familiarise and educate those living nearby and the general public who are interested enough to visit the site. The company believes the exercise has been worthwhile in removing misconceptions of the risks associated with its activities and has had the added benefit of allaying local concern and winning goodwill.

4.   Whatever objective analysis suggests, there is some research evidence to show that people expect controllable imposed risks — even small ones — to be controlled. Failure to appreciate this point has in the past caused trouble for some regulators when they have placed too much emphasis on what is a significant risk and what is not.

5.   There is a tendency on the part of some experts and commentators to draw up league tables of risks, both in terms of magnitude and probability. This may help the non-expert to gauge the magnitude of different risks but, if risk management priorities are based too strictly on position in the league, public support may be lost. Moreover, most risks are additive, whilst league tables give the impression that different risks are alternatives.

Annex 6: Relevant expert bodies

There is a wide range of bodies with expertise relevant in some degree to this guide. This annex gives details for some of the most relevant bodies and gives contact details for others whose potential relevance may be judged from their title. In addition, contacts in government Departments will be able to give further information on expert bodies.

Advisory Committee on Hazardous Substances

Address: Toxic Substances Division
          Department of the Environment
          Room A345
          Romney House
          43 Marsham Street
          London SW1P 3PY

Contact: Mr A Leverton

Tel No: 0171 276 8501
Fax No: 0171 276 8333.

The Advisory Committee on Hazardous Substances was established to advise the Secretary of State for the Environment on proposals to introduce regulations under section 140 of the Environmental Protection Act 1990; it also advises on the assessment and management of chemical substances. However, it is not able to provide advice to bodies outside Government.

There are a number of EC Regulations or Directives establishing principles for assessing the risks of new and existing chemicals. Further advice can be obtained from the above address.

Advisory Committee on Releases to the Environment

Address: Department of the Environment
Romney House
Room B351
43 Marsham Street
London SW1P 3PY

Contact: Toxic Substances Division

Tel No: 0171 276 8327
Fax No: 0171 276 8333

Description of relevance

The Advisory Committee on Releases to the Environment (ACRE) advises the Secretary of State on all applications for consents to release or market genetically modified organisms (GMOs). Such applications are made under The Genetically Modified Organisms (Deliberate Release) Regulations 1992: SI 1992 No 3280. These require applicants to supply detailed information about the GMO involved, and any intended release, and then, on the basis of the information, to carry out as assessment of the risks to the environment. Following the advice of ACRE on the key aspects of environmental risk assessment for the release of GMOs, DOE published a framework approach to risk assessment as part of the guidance to the GMO (Deliberate Release) Regulations 1992. The wider, generic approach to environmental risk assessment adopted in this guide draws extensively on the framework developed together with ACRE.

Department of the Environment

Address: Department of the Environment
Romney House
Room A329
43 Marsham Street
London SW1P 3PY

Contact: D L Perridge, Toxic Substances Division

Tel No: 0171 276 8662
Fax No: 0171 276 8333

Description of relevance

The Department's overall aim is to ensure effective protection for the environment at home and abroad. To that end environmental concerns need to be reflected in all areas of policy. The Department's specific aims for environmental protection are to:

- promote sustainable development;

- ensure prudent use of natural resources and to minimise waste;

- prevent and minimise pollution of air, land and water in cost-effective ways;

- increase informed public participation in environmental decision making and the involvement of all sectors, especially business;

- ensure environmental concerns are reflected in all the Government's work domestically and internationally;

- reduce the burden of regulation, and make markets work for the environment; and

- protect the environment, and save money, by encouraging better management methods and by promoting the cost effective use of energy in all locations.

To these ends the Department undertakes or promotes a wide range of monitoring and research; participates in international actions; promotes domestic legislation; supports inspectorates; promotes publicity and provides advice; and employs staff with relevant expertise.

Health and Safety Executive

Address: Health and Safety Executive
           Rose Court
           2 Southwark Bridge
           London SE1 9HS

Contact: Dr J M Le Guen
           Head of Risk Assessment Policy Unit

Tel No: 0171 717 6403
Fax No: 0171 717 6417

Description of Relevance

The Health and Safety Executive (HSE) enforces the Health and Safety at Work etc. Act and associated legislation covering the risks to health and safety arising in work activities. HSE's inspectors do not cover all workplaces; they cover, in general, the more serious hazards such as factories, building sites, nuclear and offshore installations etc. Local authority environmental health officers cover health and safety in places such as shops, offices and places used for leisure and consumer services.

The legal duties placed on employers (and the self-employed) are mainly goal-setting rather than prescriptive, with emphasis on the principle of 'reasonable practicability'. This principle introduces an element of proportionality, requiring the duty-holder to weigh risk against cost when deciding on control measures. Risk assessment has a pivotal role in this approach.

The legislation enforced by HSE is intended to protect workers and others (*eg* members of the public) who might be affected by work activity; little of it is concerned with protection of the environment. Notable exceptions are the Notification of New Substances Regulations and the Genetically Modified Organisms (Contained Use) Regulations, for which HSE and DOE are the joint competent authorities, and the Control of Industrial Major Accident Hazards Regulations.

HM Industrial Pollution Inspectorate (HMIPI)

Address: 27 Perth Street
          Edinburgh
          EH3 5RB

Contact: The Chief Inspector

Tel No: 0131 244 3056
Fax No: 0131 244 2903

Description of relevance

HMIPI is tasked to limit the impacts of discharges from certain industrial, commercial and public premises to the environment and uses a risk assessment based approach to identify necessary controls. Some limitations are prescribed by statute but the main regulatory thrust is based on balancing cost and environmental benefit/ disbenefit. Risk assessment is key to the application of such a methodology with the extent of the assessment being linked to the predicted hazard intensity.

It is intended that from 1 April 1996 HMIPI will be absorbed into the proposed Scottish Environmental Protection Agency (SEPA).

HM Inspectorate of Pollution

It is intended that from 1 April 1996 HMIP will be part of the proposed Environment Agency.

Address: HM Inspectorate of Pollution
Romney House
43 Marsham Street
London SW1P 3PY

Contact: Stefan Carlyle
Head of Integrated Risk Assessment
Policy Section (IRAPS)

Tel No: 0171 276 8088
Fax No: 0171 276 8562

Description of Relevance

HMIP protects the environment by enforcing regulations to prevent pollution. HMIP does this by:

- authorising and regulating high-risk (most complex and potentially seriously polluting) industrial processes;
- authorising and regulating premises where radioactive materials are used, stored or disposed of;
- regulating the production and, where appropriate, the disposal of waste from all prescribed processes;
- regulating the discharge of special category trade efficient to sewers.

HMIP also commissions research into pollution control and radioactive waste disposal technology. Risk assessment and risk management play an increasing role in the way HMIP carries out its business. This ranges from how regulatory priorities are set at a national and regional level, to the assessment of the environmental consequences of authorised releases, to how enforcement and monitoring programmes are devised and implemented. All this is designed to ensure that the Inspectorate works cost effectively to the highest professional standards.

The Medical Research Council's Institute for Environment and Health

Address: Institute for Environment and Health
University of Leicester
PO Box 138
Lancaster Road
Leicester LE1 9HN

Contact: Dr Paul T C Harrison, Programme Manager

Tel No: 0116 2525530
Fax No: 0116 2525146

Description of relevance

The Institute for Environment and Health aims to promote a healthier environment by facilitating information exchange, identifying and evaluating environmental health issues and managing research programmes on the adverse effects of chemicals, leading to a better understanding of the risk to human health and the environment from exposure to hazardous substances in air, water and soil.

IEH comprises four principal groups; a Toxicology Advisory Group, a Risk Assessment Group, an Information Unit and a Scientific Publications Unit. Key activities of the Institute are to organise meetings to which experts in relevant fields are invited to review and assess available data on given topics, to publish authoritative reviews and position documents, and to conduct and manage research projects on behalf of Government Departments and Agencies.

Ministry of Agriculture, Fisheries and Food

Address: Public Enquiry Point
3, Whitehall Place (West)
London SW1A 2HH

Contact: MAFF Helpline

Tel No: 0645 33 55 77 (local Call rate)

Description of relevance

MAFF is responsible for managing the safety of the food supply. This includes the presence of radionuclides and chemical additives and contaminants in food. The assessment of chemical risks associated with food is essentially the same as the assessment of environmental risks as outlined in this document.

Through its agencies, the Pesticides Safety Directorate and the Veterinary Medicines Directorate, MAFF is also responsible for the approval and licensing of pesticides and veterinary medicines. This process includes an environmental risk assessment.

Other environmental responsibilities of MAFF include the conservation of fish stocks, protection of the rural and marine environments, and flood prevention.

National Radiological Protection Board

Address: National Radiological Protection Board
          Chilton
          Oxon, OX11 0RQ.

Contact: Mr M C O'Riordan, Secretary

Tel No: 01235 822633
Fax No: 01235 822630

Description of relevance

The NRPB is an independent statutory body providing advice, technical services and training to national and local government, industry and the public on all aspects of ionising and non-ionising radiation. NRPB has substantial experience and expertise in many areas of risk assessment such as:

(a) the use of radiation and radioactive materials in power generation, industry, medicine and research, including waste disposal and potential accidents;

(b) natural radioactivity, notably radon in homes;

(c) exposure to electromagnetic fields; and

(d) exposure to ultra-violet radiation from the sun and man-made sources.

The capability is supported by NRPB's extensive work on personal and environmental monitoring for radiation and radioactive materials, and basic experimental research on the behaviour of radioactive materials in the environment, and on the effects of radiation on living organisms.

National Rivers Authority

Address: Rivers House
           Waterside Drive
           Aztec West
           Almondsbury
           BRISTOL, BS12 4UD

Contact: C Swinnerton, Director of Water Management and Research

Tel No: 01454 624320
Fax No: 01454 624409

Description of relevance

As the guardian of the water environment, the NRA acts as both a regulator of those who work in and use the water environment, and as an environmental manager. Increasingly, the NRA sees effective environmental management being delivered through partnerships with others having interests in the sustainable use of the water environment. The NRA's responsibilities include the protection and improvement of the water environment, the management of water resources, and the protection of people and property from flooding.

In all these activities, due consideration should be given to the assessment and management of environmental risk. The Guide provides the basis for a common understanding between the NRA and other organisations – particularly industry – of the basis of risk assessment and management, and sets out a general procedure within which an appropriate level of risk analysis can be adopted for the issues concerned.

It is intended that from 1 April 1996 the NRA will be part of the proposed Environment Agency.

Natural Environment Research Council

Address: Polaris House
           North Star Avenue
           Swindon
           SN2 1EU

Tel No: 01793 411500
Fax No: 01793 411501

The mission of the Natural Environment Research Council is:

- to promote and support, by any means, high quality basic, strategic and applied research survey, long-term environmental monitoring and related postgraduate training in terrestrial, marine and freshwater biology and Earth, atmospheric, hydrological, oceanographic and polar sciences and Earth observation;

- to advance knowledge and technology, and to provide services and trained scientists and engineers, which meet the needs of users and beneficiaries (including the agricultural, construction, fishing, forestry, hydrocarbons, minerals, process, remote sensing, water and other industries), thereby contributing to the economic competitiveness of the United Kingdom, the effectiveness of public services and policy and the quality of life;

- to provide advice on, disseminate knowledge and promote public understanding of the fields aforesaid.

Details of six NERC centres of particular relevance to this guide are given immediately below.

Centre for Coastal and Marine Sciences

Address: Plymouth Marine Laboratory
          Prospect Place
          West Hoe
          Plymouth PL1 3DH

Contact: Director CCMS
          Plymouth Marine Laboratory
          Prospect Place
          West Hoe
          Plymouth PL1 3DH

Tel No: 01752 222 772
Fax No: 01752 670 637

Description of relevance

The Centre for Coastal and Marine Sciences carries out research which is relevant across the entire spectrum of activities highlighted in this report. This research is concentrated on the coastal and shelf seas and is designed to provide quantitative information in support of modelling and of monitoring the well-being of these ecosystems in the context of impacts of industrialisation, shipping, tourism, etc. Relevant expertise includes physical, chemical and biological oceanography, integrated into models of ecosystem processes and supported by research of development into instrumentation and the requirements for data handling, archiving and presentation. The Centre is the host laboratory for a national research project into Land Ocean Interactions (LOIS) which has as its chief objective to provide water quality models in support of impact and risk assessment in the coastal zone.

Institute of Freshwater Ecology

Address: Windermere Laboratory
Far Sawrey
Ambleside
Cumbria LA22 0LP

Contact: Prof. A D Pickering
Acting Director

Tel No: 015 394 42468
Fax No: 015 394 46914

Description of relevance

The Institute provides information and expertise in many areas of risk assessment covered by this document. It conducts basic and strategic research on most aspects of the freshwater environment both in the UK and in other countries. It undertakes commissioned research for a wide range of customers in government, international and national agencies, as well as the private sector. This work contributes to wealth creation and improving the quality of life.

The research laboratories of IFE in various parts of the UK can provide advice on topics such as:

- methodologies and techniques for environmental assessment in freshwater and linked systems;

- the impact of pesticides and industrial chemicals on freshwater wildlife;

- transport rates and fate of radionuclides in lakes and reservoirs;

- effects of releasing genetically modified micro-organisms in soil and freshwater;

- the physiological responses of freshwater fish in relation to deteriorating conditions in their environment;

- the distribution of plants and animals in valued freshwater habitats;
- the environmental conditions required by freshwater species that provide fisheries of economic importance;
- risk assessment in the management of lakes and reservoirs.

The emphasis in all these topics is on the development and application of new technologies, especially mathematical models that can be used as tools by those responsible for the conservation and management of freshwater resources.

Institute of Terrestrial Ecology

Address: Monks Wood
            Abbots Ripton
            Huntingdon
            Cambridgeshire PE17 2LS

Contact: Prof. T M Roberts
            Director

Tel No: 01487 773381
Fax No: 01487 773487

Description of relevance

The Institute provides information and expertise in many of the areas of risk assessment covered by this document. It conducts basic and strategic research in all parts of the environment of the UK, and in a number of other countries. It undertakes commissioned research for a wide range of customers in government, international and national agencies and the private sector.. This work helps create wealth and improve the quality of life.

Its research centres in various parts of the UK can provide advice on:

- chemical hazard and risk assessment;
- the fate and mobility of radiochemicals;
- the impact of pesticides and industrial chemicals on wildlife;
- the distribution of plants and animals in valued habitats and in the wider countryside and town.

Risk assessment expertise extends to the environmental assessment of projects and programmes, genetically modified organisms, and the impacts of industrial accidents involving unregulated releases of chemicals in the environment.

British Geological Survey
Kingsley Dunham Centre
Keyworth
Nottingham
NG12 5GG

Tel No: 0115 9363100
Fax No: 0115 9363200

Centre for Ecology and Hydrology
Maclean Building
Crowmarsh Gifford
Wallingford
Oxon, OX10 8BB

Tel No: 01491 8388000
Fax No: 01491 832256

Unit of Comparative Plant Ecology
University of Sheffield
Sheffield
S10 2TN

Tel No: 0114 2768555
Fax No: 0114 2760159

Other Relevant Expert Bodies

Soil Survey and Land Research Centre (SSLRC)
Silsoe Campus
Silsoe
Bedfordshire
MK45 4DT

Tel No: 01525 860428 (and ask for SSLRC)

Annex 7: The origins of the precautionary principle

1.   In Chapter 2 of the book "Interpreting the precautionary principle"[1] Sonja Boehmer-Christiansen discusses the origins of the principle:

> **"The precautionary principle is said to have made its way into English during the early 1980s as the translation of the German *Vorsorgeprinzip*... In the early 1990s, *Vorsorge* became a principle which not only supports calls for strict environmental protection but also for sustainable development."**

2.   Boehmer-Christiansen later continues with an explanation:

> **"The influential 1984 Report from the Government to the Federal Parliament on the Protection of Air Quality probably gives the fullest official definition of *Vorsorge*."**

After asserting that:

> Responsibility towards future generations commands *(gebietet)* that the natural foundations of life *(natürliche Lebensgrundlagen)* are preserved *(bewahren*, a stronger if less militarist term than *schützen)* and that irreversible types of damage, such as the decline of forests, must be avoided.

Vorsorge was defined in approximate translation as follows:

> The principle of precaution commands that the damages done to the natural world (which surrounds us all) should be avoided *in advance* and in accordance with opportunity and possibility. Vorsorge further means the early detection of dangers to health and environment by comprehensive, synchronised (harmonised) research, in particular about cause and effect relationships..., it also means acting when conclusively ascertained understanding by science is not yet available. Precaution means to develop, in all sectors of the

---

[1] *Interpreting the precautionary principle.* Edited by T O'Riordan and J Cameron. Earthscan Publications Ltd, 1994. ISBN 1-85383-200-6.

economy, technological processes that significantly reduce environmental burdens, especially those brought about by the introduction of harmful substances (BMI 1984, 53).

The large number of action verbs should be noted. The principles therefore empower the state to pursue environmental precaution by four types of action, the goal being that damage must be avoided. This is the *Gebot*, or moral requirement, as distinct from *Verbot*, or government command."

3. In a report[2] prepared in 1987 at the request of the Royal Commission on Environmental Pollution, Dr Konrad von Molkte states that the *Vorsorgeprinzip* was enunciated in 1976 by the German Federal Government:

> **"Environmental policy is not fully accomplished by warding off imminent hazards and the elimination of damage which has occurred. Precautionary environmental policy requires furthermore that natural resources are protected and demands on them made with care."**

This definition includes the concept of good husbandry.

---

[2] *The Vorsorgenprinzip in West German Environmental Policy.* Royal Commission on Environmental Pollution, 12th Report, Appendix 3. 1988, HMSO. ISBN 0-10-103102-5

A8222 05/95 DDP Services

Printed in the United Kingdom for HMSO.
Dd.301432, 9/95, C20, 3396/4, 5673, 333325.